DOWN AND OUT PRAY

Down and Out Pray

Dorothy Collins

Dorothy Collins

Author of No Time for Daddy's Girl and Misfits Anonymous

ISBN: 978-1-9991691-6-9 (sc)

ISBN: 978-1-9991691-7-6 (e)

Cover designed by MiblArt.

In Memory of my late daughter Bonnie
She inspired me to publish the novels I wrote.
Thank you to my family for their support.
and
Thank you to Terry Unger in appreciation of her
encouragement and words of wisdom.

Chapter One

The young couple were so happy with the mystery of birth. Their baby had been born, a beautiful baby girl. She was all they had ever pictured. Delicate features, blonde hair, blue eyes, and a dimple in both cheeks when she smiled.

The nurse commented, "She was just born, so that would be gas."

To my husband and me, it was a smile.

Lionel had insisted on being there when the baby was coming out so that he could catch her. Dr. McIntyre's nurse had called Lionel at work to come immediately.

Lucinda's birth did not take as long as was usual for a first-born. She was anxious to get into the world. Lionel was there to help Diana to breathe through the pain. He praised her, and he tried to take the discomfort from her. Diana clung to him during her whole labor. Dr. McIntyre indicated it was time.

Lionel stepped over beside the doctor. He was in a full green surgical gown with a paper cap, paper booties, and latex gloves in anticipation. Dr. McIntyre was not happy with their decision but went along with Lionel's insistence on having this special bonding with his daughter, catching her when she was first born. His chest expanded with pride as the baby quickly slipped out of the birth canal and into his waiting hands. Lionel was a very proud father. The baby's mewing cry was almost instantaneous. Lucinda was born.

The nurse quickly took the baby from him, wrapping her in a blanket while the doctor cut the cord and completed his task.

Lionel had gone to his wife to kiss her. "Diana, she is so perfect. The feeling I got from helping her to be born, you have no idea how close a bond that will be for us." He kissed Diana. "Thank you for a perfect baby girl."

The nurse took the baby over to the proud parents. Diana reached out to take the baby for a few minutes before the nurse took her away again. The nurse said, "your baby weighs 6 pounds 8 ounces."

Dr. McIntyre suggested Lionel have a coffee while they prepared Diana to go to her room.

Lionel kissed his wife when he arrived in her room. "I love you, Diana. You are perfect, and so is our baby daughter, Lucinda, as we decided."

"Lionel, I am so happy. It wasn't as bad as I thought it would be. I love our little girl, Lucinda and you." Their declaration of love was a result of the happiness they experienced of their baby's birth. Neither of them had expressed this to each other prior to the delivery in all their five years of marriage.

"Please call my parents and yours to let them know." Diana smiled down at her baby.

"I can't wait to tell them. I will phone right away." Lionel was able to get Diana's parents but not his own. He would have to call them later. Diana's parents sent a message of congratulations for Lionel to deliver to Diana.

They gazed down at their little bundle of joy, then looked at each other with adoring smiles. Life was so perfect. Lionel wanted to leave so he could tell his parents about their new baby granddaughter. But the doctor had told the nurse he wanted to see them before Lionel left.

Lionel was on the bed with his wife and their beautiful baby shared between them. He held his wife in his arms.

This picture of the perfect family struck the doctor. Their happiness was shining through. They would need their love for each other after he imparted the sad news to them.

The pediatrician had examined the baby at Dr. McIntyre's request.

"I am Dr. Sawyer. I am a pediatrician. I asked you both to be together so I could tell you how perfect your daughter is. She is going to be a beauty when she grows up." He paused.

Lionel and Diana exchanged loving looks.

The doctor continued, "except there is a slight problem with her legs. The indication is they may be malformed in some way."

Lionel leaped to his feet. "What do you mean, malformed? You just said she was perfect. I caught her when she was born. She was perfect. How can you say she is malformed?"

"Well, on closer inspection, I found evidence of a problem with her legs. We won't know how serious it is until her bones grow and get stronger. It may be minor, or it may mean an operation. Her bones are too soft now to know for sure. We can only hope that it is minor. I am sorry to have to tell you but Dr. McIntyre thought I should see her and give you my findings."

"You can't be serious. The baby is so perfect. I saw her." Lionel wasn't rational.

"I am sorry. I am not wrong. I have to tell you about my findings. We will watch the baby's progress as she grows. Then we will know for sure. I can recommend a good specialist for her when she develops more if it is necessary."

Diana was crying. Lionel was still raging.

"Mrs. Cardwell, you have a beautiful baby. She is healthy in every other way."

"A Gimp. How can you call her beautiful? How can you say she is healthy?" Lionel yelled. Diana continued to cry, wrapping her baby in her arms as if to protect her from Dr. Sawyer's findings. She had flinched when Lionel called their baby girl a gimp.

"How can I tell my parents that they have a gimp for a granddaughter?" Lionel's words held an actual sneer.

Dr. Sawyer wanted to smash his fist into Lionel's mouth. Couldn't he see how he was wounding his wife? "Mr. Cardwell, she does not have a disability. We just have to wait. If there is a problem, then a specialist will correct it. You are hurting your wife with your unreasonable behavior."

"I knew she couldn't produce a perfect child. She is so lacking in backbone. I should have known." Lionel had now placed the baby's possible deformity on his wife.

Gone was the blissful couple. This man had no resemblance to the man who had been hugging his wife and baby. Instead, he verbally attacked his wife when the imperfection could be a part of his genes.

Before the doctor could calm the irate father, Lionel stocked out of the room without a further glance at his wife and baby.

A nurse hurried in. "Doctor, is there a problem? Mr. Cardwell is out there, yelling he is going to sue the hospital."

"Nurse, calm down. Mrs. Cardwell needs a sedative and take the baby to the nursery."

Diana spoke for the first time. "You are not taking my baby. She is mine."

"All right, Mrs. Cardwell, you can keep her in here. But I think you need a sedative to calm you." Then nodding at the nurse to do his bidding. The nurse hurried out.

"Mrs. Cardwell, I am sorry your husband took my message the way he did. It is definitely not your fault. Besides, she may be able to overcome her problem as her bones strengthen. If not, I have told you I will recommend a good specialist to correct the situation. She doesn't have to be a gimp like your husband implied."

The nurse hustled back in with the pills to sedate her. Diana didn't want to take them, but Dr. Sawyer stood over her until she did. He stood by the bed, watching Diana hug her baby, crooning to Lucinda through her tears.

Speaking to the parents about possible defects was the part of his job he hated. The task of giving parents unpleasant news during their exaltation over the wonders of the birth.

Diana's voice was fading as the pills worked their magic on this tearful mother with her beautiful baby clutched to her breast. First, her eyes closed, then opened, then closed, her hands upon the baby loosened.

Dr. Sawyer removed the baby and gave it to the nurse. "Mrs. Cardwell is to have her baby whenever she requests. Would you please pass that information on to the nursery? No, I think it best to have the baby housed in here with her at all times instead. The nursery is only to keep the baby until the sedative wears off."

Under the circumstances, he thought this was best from the mother's statement. 'You are not taking my baby. She is mine.'

Dr. Sawyer followed the nurse out of the room. He was walking to the elevator when he heard yelling at the nurse's station. He knew it was Mr. Cardwell. So, he changed direction and headed that way.

"Mr. Cardwell, will you accompany me to my office, please?"

Lionel rounded on him.

"I am demanding that the hospital take responsibility for my daughter's condition. She was fine when she was born. I saw her. Dr. McIntyre or the nurse must have done something to her." Lionel snapped at him.

"Mr. Cardwell, we will discuss this in my office. That is my decision, and I mean now." His voice held forceful authority. Then he turned away from Lionel, expecting him to follow which Lionel did, but not meekly. He was still yelling threats of malpractice and suing.

When Dr. Sawyer had Lionel in his office, he excused himself while he got the administrator to come and listen to Lionel's complaints. Dr. Sawyer could have phoned from his office, but he chose to contact Mr. Gerard from another phone. He wanted to make him aware of the situation before he came in contact with the rants of Mr. Cardwell.

When they arrived back in his office, they were both stunned to hear him saying into the phone. "Father, tell mother Diana has had the baby, but it died in childbirth."

"No, Diana is okay. But she may need quite a while to get over the death of our baby. It was a little girl." "I don't know why she died. They haven't told us."

Dr. Sawyer got over his stunned reaction and walked purposely into the room. He removed the phone from Lionel, plunking it down on the cradle on the desk.

"How dare you tell your parents your baby died. She is alive and will be a very healthy baby."

"That baby will never leave this hospital in my wife's arms or mine. That baby will be left behind. Your malpractice caused her condition, and you can deal with her for the rest of her life. And may it be a short one," Lionel retorted.

"Mr. Cardwell, your wife will not leave this hospital without the baby. So, you have to face up to your responsibilities."

"I think not. Diana will do as I say. She has no choice in the matter. I will not accept that gimpy baby, and you can't make me either. So, I will sign the papers right now to put her up for adoption."

Lionel whipped around to the administrator. "You prepare the papers right now. I want them signed before I leave here, along with the paper stating the hospital was negligent in her birth."

"Mr. Cardwell, there will be no papers. You will leave the hospital. You owe your parents an apology. They have the right to know that the baby is alive. Mr. Gerard will escort you to the door and your car if necessary." Dr. Sawyer nodded to Mr. Gerard and walked out.

"Mr. Cardwell, there will be no papers today or ever. So, you might as well go home. However, it would be best if you reflected on the events here. I know once you have had time to think it over, you will change your mind. Now, shall I escort you to your car or just to the door?" Mr. Gerard was not a big man, but he had a no-nonsense manner that commanded compliance.

Lionel walked out with him without any further verbal outbreaks of rage. Mr. Gerard stood watching until Mr. Cardwell reached his car.

Chapter Two

As the day passed, Diana was blissfully holding her baby. She gave the biggest smile when Dr. Sawyer appeared. He knew then that Diana would never give up her baby. So, he was happy with his decision for the baby to be in the room with her.

"Have you tried breastfeeding your baby yet, Mrs. Cardwell?"

"Yes, she took to the breast easily. She is a very bright girl. I just know it," Diana said proudly

"I agree. I think Lucinda is very bright. Now, I don't want you fretting over her legs. It may turn out to be nothing serious. When she develops her bones more, we will examine her again. Then the problem I foresee may have disappeared. Then I will be very sorry I have caused this upset for you and your husband. I would be remiss in my duty, however, if I didn't let you know and prepare you for potential problems."

His speech was to console her only. With his knowledge, he knew the beautiful baby could not develop her legs like a normal baby. He was confident that a specialist could alleviate the problem. Then she would walk and run normally. They would have to keep watching her progress.

"Mrs. Cardwell, have you heard from your husband?"

"No, he never came back. He is too upset. He will be fine if he is given time."

Dr. Sawyer was relieved to hear her prophecy, but he doubted that it was accurate for one minute. Mr. Cardwell didn't seem to be the forgiving kind. He wouldn't accept this infliction that marred his baby's early life.

"Mrs. Cardwell, I'm going to have a special nurse assigned to you until you leave the hospital. She will help you with the baby. In addition, she will give you suggestions for the baby's comfort."

"Is that usual?" Diana inquired.

"No, but your baby is special. So, I want to treat her that way while you are here." He avoided telling her that it was to protect her since her husband's threats to put the baby up for adoption. The anger he observed in Lionel could have some more consequences.

"If you have any problems, doubts, or anything, just tell the nurse. She will contact me right away. Now, you lay back and relax. Try to get some sleep while your baby is sleeping. She probably will need to be fed about every two hours at first." He took her hand and squeezed it gently. "I have other patients to see, but I will be available if you need me."

"Thank you, Dr. Sawyer. Thank you for your kindness. Lucinda and I will be fine. I know it. I have been preparing for this for a long time. I have wanted children since I was a teen."

"Your welcome. I know you both will be fine. Now get some sleep before Lucinda gets hungry again." Dr. Sawyer left the room with a feeling of desolation. He knew her husband wasn't a forgiving man, nor would he accept any imperfection from his behavior.

**

A calm presided over the hospital room until noon the next day. Lionel arrived. He didn't even greet his wife or baby. He just stood in the doorway and blared. "Diana, get dressed. I am taking you home. We are leaving this place right now." He walked over to the cupboard and removed her suitcase with her clothes.

"Lionel, I can't leave. I need to be released first. The baby isn't ready to go home."

"Diana, you will get dressed. You will leave here without that baby. Now here are your things." Lionel had opened her suitcase and was throwing her clothes on the bed.

The nurse who had been sitting in the chair observing things made a hasty retreat. Dr. Sawyer had been afraid of this type of action, assigning the in-room nurse to Mrs. Cardwell in case.

"Lionel, I can't leave. You are being ridiculous. Think about what you are saying. I thought you would realize your mistake by now and come back to say you loved our baby. The baby is important for us and our marriage."

"Diana, I am not going to tell you again. I want you to get dressed. We are leaving. That is all I have to say on the matter." Lionel started shoving the clothes in her hands.

Diana kept her hands fisted so that she couldn't accept her clothes.

"Lionel, I am staying here until the doctor releases me. Then Lucinda and I will be leaving together. Is that clear enough for you?" She pushed him away with her fists.

"Diana, I mean for you to get dressed because, when I leave here, you are coming with me. If you don't, then that will be the end. You and your baby will have to find somewhere else to live. You will obey me, or you will be on your own. There is no other option." Lionel's jaw was rock hard with conviction.

Diana knew that look. But she still wasn't about to give in. Lucinda was hers. If he didn't want the baby, then Lionel didn't care for her enough that she would stay with him.

Dr. Sawyer and Mr. Gerard arrived in the room. "Mr. Cardwell, your wife is not leaving here. Do we have to get security to have you removed?" Mr. Gerard was firm.

"No, I am leaving, but Diana will be staying. I have given her the option. She has decided she wants that imperfect baby rather than me. So be it. She will have to find a place to live as she won't be coming into my home with that baby. Diana, you are making a grave mistake." Lionel threw angry looks at everyone in the room.

"Lionel, I think you better leave. I will call my parents when it is time to go." Diana's voice was relatively calm. Dr. Sawyer was proud of her.

"Well, don't be calling my parents. They think your baby is dead." He glared at Diana, then turned and walked out of the room in anger after throwing this latest news at his wife.

Diana looked like he had shot her. Her mouth was forming a no, but no sound came out.

Dr. Sawyer walked over to her. "I am afraid that is true. We heard him on the phone yesterday, telling his parents the baby had died. I'm so sorry. He also intended to have the baby put up for adoption so it would be out of your lives," he said sadly. "Just maybe when he has time to think about things, he will change his mind."

"I don't think so. Lionel is not a man to change his mind once he has said something. I have made too many concessions for a peaceful marriage over the years, but not this time. How could he tell anyone Lucinda died? That is beyond forgiveness for me. I will never enter his house again. Especially not since he made that horrible announcement to his parents and now to me. That is too much for me to forgive. Lucinda is mine. I intend to keep her." Diana began to cry. Lionel had wounded her heart forever. She and Lucinda would get along fine without him.

Dr. Sawyer placed his hand on her shoulder. To bolster her spirits, he offered, "we will help you find a place to live. You can count on that. You will be fine." He stroked her back as Diana started to weep.

Lucinda had awakened during the yelling. The nurse tried to soothe her until Diana could attend to her baby. Mr. Gerard looked on helplessly.

A nurse ran into the room. "Mr. Gerard, you are needed immediately downstairs. Some crazy man is turning over chairs and tables in the lobby, ranting and raving at the hospital."

Mr. Gerard took off immediately. As he ran, he called for security with his two-way radio, which he kept clipped to his belt for such emergencies.

Diana cried all the more with this news. Lionel was out of her life now and forever after this. Lucinda, her baby, was what she wanted. She had been willing to overlook all his many faults, which she had discovered after they were married. He had treated her so differently when he first met her. Now she had to face reality. Life with Lionel would never be easy.

She couldn't do that to Lucinda, forcing her baby into a stringent atmosphere with Lionel. He was always very strict with herself and later would be with Lucinda.

It finally penetrated her mind, Lucinda's loud crying, needing her. Diana pulled away from Dr. Sawyer's caring hand.

"I'll be all right now. Lucinda needs me. I need to look after her right now." Diana's voice was quite firm.

This woman had accepted the situation much better than her husband. Dr. Sawyer had to praise her for her strong will. He knew then that Diana would never give up her baby, nor would she go back to her husband.

Dr. Sawyer looked at the nurse.

"Nurse, Mrs. Cardwell needs her baby. You can give Lucinda to her now."

Diana was holding out her arms, waiting for her beautiful baby that was hers alone now.

She cooed to the baby as she bared her breast. The baby found the nipple.

Diana raised her tear-stained face to Dr. Sawyer. "We will be okay now. Lucinda and I have each other." Diana smiled weakly at him. Then her smile widened as she gazed down at Lucinda. The nurse eased a pillow under her arm for comfort.

**

Despite all the trouble Lionel tried to cause for the hospital, Diana was not deterred from undertaking her new role in her life.

However, the worst day was when Lionel's parents showed unannounced, only to find her feeding the baby. She was embarrassed at the intimacy of her exposed breast. She didn't feel she had been very close to them.

Then the horror set in when they discovered their granddaughter was still alive. How could Lionel have done this to his parents?

They had never been close to Lionel, nor had Lionel made trips to see them. But they certainly didn't deserve this type of shock from their son.

"Diana, you have a baby." Lionel's mother exclaimed.

"Yes, a baby girl, which we named Lucinda." Diana was not going to lead the conversation. She was embarrassed enough with her exposed breast and their eyes focused on the baby-making suckling mewing sounds. Diana wished she had something to throw over her shoulder.

"But Lionel phoned us. He said the baby had died. Why would he do that?" Lionel's father asked in an unpleasant voice.

"I don't know. You will have to ask Lionel about that." Lucinda had stopped feeding. She slipped her breast away from Lucinda's mouth and pulled her nightie closed. She maneuvered the baby around. So, they could see her pretty little face with her lips still moving in a sucking motion.

"My, she is a pretty elfin, isn't she?" Her mother-in-law had moved over to the bed. "Lucinda is a pretty name. I think it suits her."

Her father-in-law never approached the baby. Instead, he just said, "come, Matilda, we have to find Lionel. Evidently, there is a problem here. We have to get to the bottom of this immediately. Come," he ordered.

Diana cringed. That was precisely how Lionel spoke to her on occasion. He had been emulating his father, and she had never been aware of it.

"Would you like to hold her, Mother Matilda?" as she always had been instructed to call her.

"Yes, I would, but only for a second, then we must go," she said meekly, not looking at her husband, who was making harrumphing sounds to command her obedience.

Mother Matilda took the baby. She smiled down at the little face, that sweet mouth still moving and adoring her downy fuzz of shiny blonde hair covering her little head.

"She is so pretty, Diana. Why would Lionel refuse this child?"

"Matilda, give the baby back to her. We are leaving now."

Matilda gave the baby back to Diana, which pleased her. She enclosed the baby protectively in her arms from the gruff-voiced father-in-law still lamenting they should leave.

He advanced on his wife. A weak goodbye from Mother Matilda as her father-in-law dragged her with him to the door.

Diana's arms locked tighter around her baby. They could not hurt her, and neither would Lionel. She made a firm commitment to protecting Lucinda, no matter what. Diana intended not to have any more dealings with Lionel, not that he would try. She knew for sure now. He would never accept his daughter.

Dr. Sawyer was concerned when he came in. "How are you doing? I hear you had visitors. I understand they were your husband's parents."

"Yes, they were shocked to see the baby. They wanted an explanation. I told them to ask Lionel. My mother-in-law held the baby for a moment. But Lionel's father never came near us. You know, doctor, I never realized until now that Lionel was so much like his father. So many Europeans demand obedience from a woman. Although Lionel was born here., he still has the same trait to have unquestionable obedience." Diana's voice held awe at the enlightenment.

"Yes, I have noticed some Europeans acting that way on occasion. His parents didn't say anything to hurt you, did they?"

"No, I never gave them a chance. I just told them to ask Lionel. He must give them an explanation. You know, I am glad this happened, not Lucinda's legs but the breakup of our marriage. Under her father's influence, Lucinda would have a hard life. He was rather a stern demanding man. Lionel changed after I married him. He seemed to be such a gentleman when he dated me. After, I had to keep making excuses for his behavior to my family and business friends. I can see that now."

"Well, I don't normally support single parents. It is so beneficial for both parents to be together in raising a child. But I can see that one parent might be the case for Lucinda. So, I will help you find shelter when you leave here."

"I could always go to my parents. They would help me. But I don't think I could get a job there. They live in a small town which doesn't offer much work potential. So, I will need to be in the city for job opportunities."

"Diana, you mustn't worry about work right away. I will find something for you, at least temporarily, until you get stronger. Do you have work experience that will make getting a job easy?"

"Not really. Lionel wanted me to quit my job when we married. He wanted me to be there for him when he came home. Being the money provider was important to him. He didn't like career women much. As I wanted a baby so badly, I complied. But it took five years. So, I have been away from work that long," she finished lamely.

Lucinda was crying. She was fussing because her feeding time had been interrupted. Diana was reluctant to expose her breast in front of Dr. Sawyer.

Their relationship had changed now that he had taken a personal interest in her and her baby. Dr. Sawyer soon recognized this.

"Diana, I will go check out those arrangements that I mentioned, and then I will be back." He left the room quickly. Why had he started addressing her as Diana?

He had gone from doctor to friend because he wanted to help her personally. There was something about her situation that had touched his heart. He had lost his detachment to this patient, a definite no-no.

Maybe it was because Diana was a brave woman to face her situation the way she had. He admired her for that. Lucinda deserves better than a man like Lionel. How dare he call that beautiful baby a gimp. That distasteful word didn't apply to Lucinda.

He knew he was getting too involved in this woman's life. But he couldn't help himself. She was getting such a raw deal. How could he not get involved? What started out as being a protective influence to stop her husband became so much more for him.

He was going to ask his sister, Lucy if she would take Diana in for a while. He would help pay her expenses.

Dr. Sawyer made a point each year of helping someone out. He felt that was the best way to give back to the community for his successful practice. This year Diana and Lucinda would be his project. He intended to keep an eye on them.

Over the past months, he was helping his sister to heal over the loss of her husband and son in a car accident eighteen months ago. She found the house so big and empty without them. Lucy was inclined to get depressed at times. She worked out of her home, so she didn't even get away from it during business hours. He was sure Diana wouldn't mind sharing Lucinda with his sister. That way, they would be helping each other to alleviate their problem. As soon as he got back to his office, he put in a call to his sister.

"Hi, Lucy. Busy?"

“Never too busy for my little brother. What do you want to do tonight?”

He made a point of stopping by once a week for a gabfest with her.

“I thought we could go out for Chinese food. I want to butter you up before I spring my surprise on you.”

“That sounds ominous. I have a feeling you want to do something I may regret saying yes to. What is it this time, Troy? A stray cat or dog?”

“Not until I have you mellow over dinner. You will have to be patient until then.”

“All right,” Lucy laughed. “So that you know, I am not taking in any stray pets. The last time, it was a Great Dane, and he dragged me all over the place.” Lucy was barely five feet tall and petite.

So, he understood the Great Dane was an unwise pet for her. He had talked a male friend into taking the dog instead.

“You will have to wait. See you at seven. Try to be ready for a change,” Troy chuckled.

His sister was one of those women who were perpetually late.

Troy leaned back in his chair, thinking about Diana and Lucinda installed in Lucy’s house. Perhaps, Diana could do the cooking and light housekeeping for her keep. Unfortunately, Lucy was a very poor cook. She wasn’t a domestic person at all. So, this would be the perfect arrangement.

Troy felt sure Diana wouldn’t agree to this unless he presented it as a way to help his undomesticated sister from being buried under the clutter. Then the thought struck him what if Diana couldn’t cook either. Troy chuckled at the thought.

Chapter Three

Dr. Sawyer's happy thoughts were interrupted as the phone rang. It was the special nurse for Diana. "Mr. Cardwell came in and has bodily taken his wife from the hospital wrapped in a blanket. He left the baby behind."

Dr. Sawyer inquired, "did you call security?"

"Yes, they are checking the hospital, and the informed police have arrived."

Dr. Sawyer left his office at a run. He had to get back to the hospital. When he arrived, he found several police officers in front of the hospital entrance. He parked his car then raced inside.

Mr. Gerard was wringing his hands in agitation. Ever since the Cardwell baby was born, this hospital had become a place of high emotions, threats, and kidnapping. He fervently wished for the Cardwell baby's placement with the Children's Aid Society social worker. Then, his usual quiet hospital could then return to its typical peaceful existence.

Dr. Sawyer asked Mr. Gerard, "have they found Mr. and Mrs. Cardwell?"

"No, not yet. We know he took the stairway at the East side of the hospital. So, we are assuming Mr. Cardwell successfully made his escape. The police are questioning people in the hopes of someone witnessing their departure. But I don't know whether they have been successful. I am still waiting to hear."

Upon finding Diana's room empty, Dr. Sawyer raced to the nursery. He relaxed, seeing the peaceful sleeping baby Lucinda, unaware of the dramatic escape by her parents. Changing direction, Dr. Sawyer went looking for Nurse Spiegel. He found her at the nurse's station near Diana's room.

"Tell me exactly what happened." Dr. Sawyer demanded of Nurse Spiegel.

"Mrs. Cardwell had just fed the baby and returned her to her bassinet. Then she got back into bed, laying back to have a little nap. I straightened the covers around her for a nice quiet time. Then Mr. Cardwell rushed into the room. He didn't say a word. He just raced over to the bed.

Mrs. Cardwell was asleep, so she didn't even realize Lionel was there. He tucked the covers around her so she couldn't move and raced out of the room. He had her face tight against his chest, so she couldn't even call out.

I tried to block his way, but he dug his elbow into me viciously. I had to step back and allow him to run out of the room. When I recovered my breath, I ran after them, yelling for help. But he must have ducked down the stairwell because we couldn't find him," she paused for breath.

"I should have realized where he had gone because it didn't take me long to recover from his attack. Yet when I came out of the room, they were nowhere in sight. All I could think about was getting help. I'm sorry."

"It is not your fault, getting help was the best way to handle the situation. If he left by the side stairwell to get away, that would take him away from the parking lot. He would have to cross one of the other floors. We will have to find out which floor he used. Someone must have seen him."

The elevator opened. Two police officers emerged and headed for the nursing station.

"Which room was Mrs. Cardwell in? Who saw what happened?"

Dr. Sawyer said, "Nurse Spiegel was in the room at the time. Mr. Cardwell jabbed her with his elbow when she tried to stop him."

"Which one is Nurse Spiegel?" looking towards the three nurses.

A nurse stepped forward. "I am Nurse Spiegel. I was the one in the room at the time."

"Would you like to show me the room?"

The two officers, along with Nurse Spiegel and Dr. Sawyer, trooped down to the empty room.

While the officers were looking around, the slighter man said, "I am Officer Jackson, and this is Officer Thompson," fluttering his hand toward his fellow officer. "There doesn't appear to be any sign of a struggle." Although, the hospital bed was void of covers except for the bottom sheet and the scattered pillows.

Officer Jackson, who seemed to be the spokesman, asked Nurse Spiegel if she would be more comfortable sitting. She refused the offer and repeated her story in a concise voice. Officer Jackson was making brief notes as she talked.

Then he turned to Dr. Sawyer. "Is there something you would like to add to fill me in on this picture?"

"Yes, I am Dr. Sawyer, her pediatrician. Dr. McIntyre delivered her baby, which was a normal birth. Mr. Cardwell aided in the delivery as he wanted a special closeness with his baby. A bonding process in his mind, Dr. McIntyre mentioned."

"Dr. McIntyre asked me to check the baby, which is a normal procedure. She is a beautiful baby in every way. Except I discovered her legs were sort of twisted, which is not natural. I had seen this condition once before that corrected easily with surgery. However, this one wasn't as severe, and because the bones are pliable at birth, they could straighten on their own." He paused, letting this be absorbed before continuing. He straightened his shoulders and continued.

"It was my sad duty to tell the couple about the baby's legs and the faint possibility of an operation in the future. Not a task that I like at all. Mrs. Cardwell was stunned and accepting, but Mr. Cardwell was not." He paused.

"Here, this couple was in perfect jubilation with each other and their baby. I had to spoil this family's happiness. Mr. Cardwell was on the bed with his arms around his wife and baby when I entered the room. After I gave them the news, Mr. Cardwell shot off the bed, yelling."

"My baby is perfect. I saw her delivered. I caught her. She was perfect in every way.' Then Mr. Cardwell switched to – 'the hospital must have done something to her after the delivery.' reducing the wife to tears." Dr. Sawyer recalled Lionel's obnoxious behavior as he continued.

"He continued ranting. Then he left the room, demanding to see someone. He was accusing the hospital of doing something to his baby when he was out at the nurse's station. I tried to calm Mrs. Cardwell by giving her a sedative.

Then I took Mr. Cardwell to an office available to me when I needed privacy to discuss patients. I left him alone to get Mr. Gerard, our Administrator. When we returned to the office, we found Mr. Cardwell on the phone talking to his parents. He was telling them the baby had died at birth.

The message shocked both Mr. Gerard and me, making me angry. I grabbed the phone from him and plunked it down. Lucinda is his beautiful daughter, and he was denouncing her. He even called her a gimp. She didn't deserve talk like that," said Dr. Sawyer with clenched fists.

Officer Jackson took note of Dr. Sawyer's fury. "Go ahead. What happened then?"

"Mr. Gerard and I tried to reason with him. But he was demanding to sign papers to be drawn up by the hospital. Adoption papers for his daughter and papers stating the hospital's responsibility for his perfect daughter's change into a gimp. His words, not mine," Dr. Sawyer added, "Lucinda, the baby will never be a gimp. I hate that word."

"I understand. Go on. What happened next?"

"We told Lionel there would be no papers to sign. We directed Mr. Cardwell to go home and think about it constructively. But he arrived back the next day in Diana's . . . Mrs. Cardwell's room, demanding that she dress and leave the hospital."

The two police officers exchanged looks at the name change. Both had noticed the slip. Was there more to this than they were aware of?

Dr. Sawyer picked up his story.

"I ordered Nurse Spiegel to stay in her room because of the husband's defiance and the possibility of his sudden appearance. So, she called for reinforcements to deter Mr. Cardwell from forcing his wife to dress and leave the next day. Lionel wanted her to leave without the baby. Mr. Gerard dissuaded him and escorted him out of the hospital. Then he came back today and physically carried her out wrapped in her blankets."

"Well, that is quite a story. Where is the baby now? May we see her?" flipping his notebook closed.

"Yes, the baby is in the nursery. I will take you there." Dr. Sawyer headed out of the room with the two officers trailing behind him.

"Dr. Sawyer, if Dr. McIntyre is her doctor, how come you are so involved?"

Dr. Sawyer stopped, turning towards Officer Jackson. "Only because I was there to impart the news that caused all the uproar in the first place. I was trying to reassure Mr. Cardwell not to feel this way about the baby. I will be keeping an eye on the baby's progress as her legs mature to see what would be necessary for a corrective procedure. I told him about one baby I attended that had been born with a broken nose. The bones in his nostrils were completely twisting the nose sideways. The nose straightened within a couple of weeks. So, these things do happen. Their bones are so soft at birth, and they are pliable. But he wouldn't listen."

"Is Dr. McIntyre aware of what's going on?"

"Yes, I have kept in touch with Dr. McIntyre, keeping him abreast of the situation. He figured that with my knowledge of Lucinda's condition, I should stay in the picture rather than him."

Officer Jackson started walking. They continued towards the nursery.

"Would you mind waiting at the window? I will arrange for the nurse to bring Lucinda over." Dr. Sawyer went through the door to speak with the nurse then returned to stand with the officers.

The nurse held up the baby for them to see. Officer Thompson said, "babies are usually funny looking when they are born, I hear. But she is beautiful." His voice held awe. "How could a father reject this baby?"

"My sentiments exactly," said Dr. Sawyer.

The nurse unwrapped the baby so that they could see her fully. The baby's legs were at a slightly odd angle to normal, but not too much. Officer Jackson had expected something much worse, like club feet or something. The nurse rewrapped the baby.

"She is a little doll. Mr. Cardwell is unrealistic," Dr. Sawyer said in a warm voice.

"Yes, she is a cutie. That man needs to correct his way of thinking." Officer Jackson stated factually. "I have to tell you things don't look good. I haven't had any calls from my men, so I believe he got away. We will stay for a while, getting information from witnesses. But I think we should be searching his home and talking to relations."

"I know if Mrs. Cardwell gets the opportunity, she will be back for her baby," stated Dr. Sawyer.

"I believe that too. Is there any possibility that Mrs. Cardwell will be able to change his mind?" inquired Officer Jackson.

"No, I don't think so. I have noticed so far, Mr. Cardwell controls her pretty much."

"That is a shame. Well, we will post a guard near the nursery just in case. Otherwise, we should be on our way. Thank you for all your help, Dr. Sawyer."

"Can you keep me posted? I would really like to help Mrs. Cardwell if I could. She mentioned that she has decided to leave her husband after his unforgivable behavior of saying the baby died at childbirth to his parents and accusing her of birthing an imperfect baby. I have arranged a place for the baby and her at my sister's. Lucy is willing to take Diana in. Diana would be able to earn her keep by doing light housework until she feels fit enough to go out and get a job." Dr. Sawyer was anxious about dropping Diana's formal name. But he wanted to know what was happening. Could her husband be physically hurting her?

"Yes, I'll keep you informed. That baby needs her mother. I am sure she will be grateful for your arrangements for her and the baby. If she manages to get away from her husband, that is." The officers said their goodbyes, walking off at a quick pace. Both anxious to be out there looking for the parents.

Officer Thompson commented as they walked along. "That baby is so adorable. How could a father walk away from her?"

"Some men can't stand imperfections at all. He probably thinks it is a blight on his manhood. No wonder the wife didn't want to go with him. That type of man will never see reason or change his mind even given time."

When they reached their police cruiser, Officer Thompson asked, "where to first?"

"Let's try their home. I got the address from the hospital, 72 Lawton Road. It is not too far from the hospital."

"Yeah, I know where it is. My sister's cleaning lady lived on Lawton. I drove her home once when it was raining."

As they approached the house, there was no sign of a car. They parked a few places away.

"You go around the back, and I will go to the front. I doubt that Mr. Cardwell will have a gun. Be careful just in case," Officer Jackson ordered.

He went to the front door. He knocked, but there was no answer. Trying the door handle, it turned. He eased it open cautiously, creeping inside. "This is the police," he spoke loudly, but only silence greeted him. He continued looking in every room as he made his way to the back of the house. The kitchen showed signs of someone living there. There were boxes of food and tins piled haphazardly on the counter. Either they bought groceries and never put them away, or they were bought expressly for packing and never packed. Maybe not taking the time if his wife wasn't being cooperative.

Officer Jackson continued down the hall after letting Officer Thompson in through the kitchen door, saying, "no one is here, but I get the feeling they did come home." Upon reaching the first bedroom, made into a nursery, they noticed things were chaotic. Baby clothes, baby oils, and powder spilled on the floor. The yellow crib blanket scattered on top had sopped up the oil in one corner. The crib was cockeyed.

Officer Jackson knew right then that this would not be an easy situation that would end speedily. This man would never change his mind. He has turned against that bundle of joy with a vengeance.

Officer Thompson let out a sigh. "This guy is really bonkers. He isn't about to accept his baby, even given time."

"That's my sentiments too."

Continuing down to the next bedroom, they saw further evidence of Mr. Cardwell's ire, the thrown hospital blankets in the corner of the room. The bed had been slept in probably by Mr. Cardwell and not made. But what was evident was the opposite side that should be tidy had the bedspread bunched up like someone had scrunched it in their hands in fear or pain.

There were ladies' clothes pulled off hangars, trailing out of the closet. The dresser top had things knocked over. The drawers were half pulled out with panties hanging there as if waiting to be packed. Stockings were hanging precariously from another drawer. Either Mr. Cardwell had done the packing or forced his wife to pack in such a hurry, she couldn't get it all.

They found several used tissues in the bathroom, thrown in the wastebasket and on the counter. The cupboard was open. There were empty spaces as if things were gone. The used wet tissues verified Mrs. Cardwell was crying and very unhappy about the situation.

**

"Lionel, where are you taking me? I want my baby. Lucinda is such a pretty girl. Please, Lionel, I want my baby." Tears were pouring down Diana's face. She had given up trying to control them. They were falling onto her sweater, which was soaking them up greedily.

"Be quiet and quit the blubbering. We have not got a baby. The baby died at birth. You had better remember that in the future. There will be no more children, got that, Diana? We will start a new life somewhere else."

"Lionel, I will not act like my baby is dead. She is very much alive. I will always hate you for this. Let me out. I want to go back for Lucinda."

Lionel had tied her hands. Then locked the door. So, she couldn't get out when the car stopped at a red light.

"You have no baby. I told you. I saw it die at birth, remember? I will have to take you for treatments if you continue. I will tell them that you cannot accept the fact that your baby died."

Diana stared at him in horror. "You wouldn't do that. Why do you want me with you? I don't understand. Why can't you accept that I want my baby more than I want to be with you."

Lionel hit her across her mouth with the back of his hand. "I will not accept any more of that talk, do you hear me? You are my wife, and I have no baby. You will do as I say. You belong to me. There is no reason to let you go."

"Lionel, you do not own me. No one owns another human being. I will escape at the first opportunity." Again, he brought up his hand, whacking her across the mouth. This time, a man in a car observed him while waiting to pull out into traffic from the side of the road. He spotted the license plate 786DYE.

He picked up his cellphone from the seat and dialed 911, telling the female voice. "There is a man hitting a woman in a green Pontiac. The license number is 786DYE."

"No, I am not following them. I am parked on Robinson Avenue, waiting to pull out into traffic. Robinson and Third Avenue. They are still on Robinson, but I can barely see them. They are too far ahead now."

The information came over the police radio as an alert. Officers Thompson and Jackson had just gotten back in their squad car.

"Go, we are too far away to catch them. But if the police do, I want to be there," advised Jackson.

That was all Thompson needed to hear. The siren went on, and the cruiser sped down the street like it was shot from a cannon. He took the corner on two wheels, it seemed.

"Okay, Thompson, slow down. We aren't in a high-speed chase. I would like to live to interrogate this guy."

Thompson's grin widened. "Ah geez, I never get to race anymore."

"No, and you're not going to while I'm in the car."

The radio crackled to life and started squawking.

"He is just ahead. I can see him. He is at Robinson and Grand, but there are still too many cars in front of me. I don't want to put my siren on, as he may turn off in front of me." Came the staticky voice over the police radio.

Officer Jackson was trying telepathy on the police officer in the chase. *Put the siren on and clear the way.* He spoke, "I want this guy badly." Eagerness was evident in his voice.

Thompson looked at his cohort. Jackson didn't usually get too riled about many events. But for some reason, he was really getting into this case. Perhaps it was the baby. Thompson knew that Jackson and his wife wanted a baby. But, so far, they had not been fortunate enough to have one. He had mentioned once that she had a couple of miscarriages. But they were still hopeful.

The radio crackled to life again.

"I am gaining on him, but he is going to have to turn off soon. Is there anyone else in the area?"

"Yes," came another voice. "I am approaching Robinson on Stewart. Robinson ends here, so he has to go either right or left. Do you think he knows we are chasing him?"

"I don't think so. I am still too far behind the car, to be sure. Are you right or left on Stewart?"

"Left, if he takes a left, I've got him. I have turned off my siren. You said a green Pontiac license 786DYE. He is in my sight. He turned left in my direction." The dispatch came on to confirm the license number.

The cruiser was two cars back from the corner. The cop had caught the license as the Pontiac made its left turn. The cop made a quick U-turn to follow him when traffic would allow. The cop's direction now was a red light. Did he put on his siren or not? Was the guy aware of his police car? Stewart was four Lanes, so he should be able to maneuver around the two ahead. His heart was starting to pump rapidly in anticipation as the light changed. The left lane held three cars. Two of the vehicles turned left. He passed the car ahead. Now there were two cars in front, one in each lane. He was blocked. He flashed his lights, warning the car in front of him to pull over. But the car ahead doggedly kept going. He was still blocked.

The car in the left lane spotted the cruiser's flashing lights in his side mirror. He shot ahead of the guy in front of the cruiser. The cruiser moved over. He had a clear road ahead. He passed the two cars, but the suspect must have noticed too because he sped up and was going all out. The chase was on.

Chapter Four

"He is making a run for it. He must have spotted me." came an excited voice on the radio. A siren was evident in the background.

"Come on, pull over. You know I'm on your tail. It will go harder on you if you keep going, buddy." The excited voice was saying over the airwaves. "You won't outrun me. That's it, pull over. He is pulling over to the curb. I've got him." The staticky radio emitted the excited voice. The siren's pealing died.

Officer Jackson asked, "how far are we from Stewart?"

"About fifteen minutes yet."

The radio crackled to life.

"He took off while I was out of my car approaching him. I am chasing him again. But he turned off while I ran for my car. I don't know which way he went." Disappointment was evident in the officer's voice. "I have turned right on Lomas, but there is no green Pontiac. So, I will have to make a U-turn." "Now I see him in the distance. But traffic on Stewart is heavy, and I can't get through."

"I have my siren on, but I'm not getting a break in traffic. C'mon. C'mon," the voice was saying. "The other cruiser is stopping traffic. I'm through, and he is with me. We are both in pursuit. But the Pontiac is far ahead now. I'm flooring the pedal." The voice was giving instructions to the second cruiser. "You be ready to pull left, and I'll turn right as he has turned off again."

The voice instructed as he turned. "No car in sight. Take a left. He has turned that way. Do you see him?"

"No one this way either. He must've turned on the next block above. I am turning to get to the next block."

"Yeah, me too." Screeching tires came over the airwaves.

"Get him," Thompson was yelling. "You know, I think he may be heading our way. Keep your eyes peeled. Gotcha, here he comes. Darn, I can't make a U-turn properly. The road is too narrow." Thompson was doing a three-point turn.

"Hurry, keep on him. Thompson, you can speed now. You have my permission," said Officer Jackson anxiously.

"I fully intended to without your permission," came the reply.

"This guy can really drive, but we're gaining. Do you think he will pull the same trick on us?" Thompson asked excitedly.

"I'll get out of the car. You be ready to give chase. Keep on him. That's done it, he should be stopping. That truck is pulling out in front of him. God, he has hit him."

Thompson jammed on the brakes. But it was a forgone conclusion that he wouldn't be able to stop at this speed. However, he had slowed down in anticipation of the Pontiac stopping. A loud crash sounded. The cruiser hit the suspect's car on the driver's side as it spun out on impact from the truck. The airbags inflated, making it impossible for either officer to move temporarily.

"Dispatch get ambulances to Thierry and Jensen, quickly. There may have been some injuries," came the voice over the radio, "a cruiser and the suspect's car and a truck have collided." The radio went silent. The other two police cars were on the scene.

The car door opened on Officer Jackson's side. "Help me out from this damn thing," pushing the airbag away. "Are you okay, Thompson?"

"Not really," replied a painful voice.

"Well, we will get you out." Turning to the officer, "see to the other car. Assess the damage and get back to me. There is a woman and a man in that car. The woman is there under protest, so treat her kindly."

They could hear sirens now. Jackson rushed around to his partner's door. He had difficulty getting it open at first. The frame was bent off-kilter on impact.

He surmised from Officer Thompson's laments, he had cracked or broken ribs, and one leg was painful in summation. He could not help his partner anymore as he needed an ambulance that sounded like it was on its way. "Hold tight, Carl. The ambulance will soon be here to help you. I will go see how the other car passengers made out" Jackson went over to see how the other car fared.

Airbags automatically deploy on the impact of a collision, which activates powder that produces gases that activates the airbag. But for some reason, Lionel's airbag had not triggered.

Diana's face sustained injuries of cuts and bruises, and she had a broken left arm. Unlike Lionel, whose injuries seemed pretty serious. The truck driver had fared the best. He was just jolted but not injured.

The first to arrive was the fire department, followed closely behind by the police and ambulances.

It took the jaws of life to release Lionel from the wreckage. The fire department worked on getting him out. The paramedics took Diana's vital signs and stabilized her arm. Diana was crying out for her baby.

"Mrs. Cardwell, we will reunite you with your baby," said Officer Jackson firmly. He noted she never asked how Lionel was doing.

They strapped her securely on a gurney and put her into the ambulance.

Officer Jackson went back over to his partner. "Looks like Mrs. Cardwell sustained a broken arm and facial welts. Otherwise, she is okay, which is a miracle. Lionel didn't though his airbag did not deploy. Mrs. Cardwell is crying about her baby. I assured her that we would reunite her with her baby. How are you?"

"Other than my ribs and leg, I'm okay. That shouldn't keep me down long. I am glad Mrs. Cardwell is okay. All I thought about when I knew I couldn't stop was that I might kill her. She didn't deserve that. Thank heavens the car spun out, so I hit the driver's side instead. How is Lionel?" He winced in pain as the paramedics transferred him to a stretcher.

"We don't know yet. The firefighters are still trying to get him out. They tried from Mrs. Cardwell's side, but he is jammed in behind the wheel. The door is pushed in. So, they haven't been able to release him yet. He doesn't look too good. The truck driver wasn't injured, nor his truck much. The Cardwell car is probably a write-off."

"What about the cruiser?" Thompson inquired.

"Well, it needs some work. Let's put it that way. Now, lay back and relax so they can get you out of here," said Jackson as he walked beside his partner's stretcher.

He stood watching as the ambulance took off with its siren clearing the way. Then he walked over to Lionel. They had most of the door peeled away. Two paramedics anxiously waited to take the injured man into their care upon his extraction from the wreckage.

Mr. Cardwell would have other things to think about now instead of obtaining his wife or his baby. A beautiful baby he had rejected because of her legs, saying she wasn't perfect. Well, Mr. Cardwell, you aren't perfect either anymore. Strange how fate stepped in, deeming that Mr. Cardwell wouldn't be perfect either. Usually, he felt terrible for the car crash victims, but he couldn't feel that way for Lionel. He didn't deserve his sympathy.

One of the officers came over to get his statement. It was the officer that had helped him out of the damaged police car.

"I noticed that you assessed the damage, so I didn't get back to you. I want to ask you. Is there anything you want to add to my report? I know you will be filing a report on this incident too."

"Yes, I want it to go on record that Officer Thompson tried his best to avoid contact with the fleeing car. But after the car hit the truck, it spun around right towards us. So, we had no other option but to come in contact with the Pontiac. It looks like Mrs. Cardwell is not too badly off, considering the extent of the damage to the car. I am glad of that."

"Yes, she is going to be okay, but Mr. Cardwell won't fare so well." He had taken part in the chase, and he was curious as to the reason. "So, what's the story there anyway?"

"He was kidnapping his wife. She just delivered a beautiful baby a couple of days ago. The baby's legs might have a problem. The big word is 'might,' according to the baby's doctor. The husband deemed her imperfect, accusing the hospital of malpractice because he couldn't accept the baby was flawed. He told his parents the baby had died. Also, he insisted his wife abandon the baby at the hospital. But, of course, she wants the baby. Mr. Cardwell called their baby a gimp. Well, who is the gimp now?" Jackson's voice reflected his ire at Mr. Cardwell.

The officer looked with renewed feelings towards the car where the firefighters were working. Anyone who would abandon a baby was scum, in his opinion, thinking about his love for his own two little girls. The way they ran to him when he arrived home, laughing and giggling, both trying to hug and kiss him at once.

He expressed, "it doesn't look like this guy will be Mr. Perfect now, does it?"

"No, I agree. Unfortunately, Mr. Perfect is like Humpty Dumpty. He had a great fall, and I doubt they will be able to put him together again as perfect as he would like to be," Officer Jackson said emphatically.

The firefighters lifted Mr. Cardwell out of the car. He had passed out into oblivion. The paramedics stabilized his neck, put him on a board in case of back injuries. One paramedic hooked him up to an IV and oxygen while the other took his vital signs. Then, Lionel was being lifted onto the stretcher by the firefighters.

Tow trucks appeared. The crowd was kept back by stern officers now that the accident scene was secured.

The police obtained statements from witnesses and the truck driver.

The victim was secured and transferred. Lionel's ambulance wailing siren screeched into the air. Cars pulled over to give it passage along the streets on its trip to Emergency.

Officer Jackson directed the 'chase' officer to give him a ride into the hospital after there appeared to be no reason to stay.

Arriving at the hospital, he first went in search of details on Mrs. Cardwell. He found she was back in her hospital bed with her baby in her arms. The baby was feeding. Nurse Spiegel quickly covered her with a light baby's blanket as she noted his presence in the doorway.

Officer Jackson observed that Nurse Spiegel was fluttering around Mrs. Cardwell, trying to make her comfortable. Her arm was now in a cast, resting on one pillow and another under the arm with the baby. So, the mother was as comfortable as possible.

Diana smiled through her battered face. The contusions were a deep red from the car accident.

"Mrs. Cardwell, it is nice to see you reunited with your baby. I am Officer Jackson. I am sorry to say that I was in the police cruiser that hit your husband's car. We tried, but we couldn't stop enough when your husband's car spun out of control. So, in a way, we feel responsible for your injuries. I am so sorry that you were injured."

"I am so happy to be back with Lucinda that I haven't let my injuries bother me. I am just thankful that you found us. Lionel had no idea where we were going. He was leaving town with no destination. I kept asking him to stop. I didn't want to leave my baby. He kept hitting me when I said that."

"So, all these facial bruises aren't a result of the accident?"

"No, Lionel wears a ring on his right hand. He kept backhanding my face. How did you find us so soon?"

"Well, Mrs. Cardwell, there was a concerned citizen that saw your husband hitting you. He called 911. We already had a description of your car. So, when the man identified your car, we were already out there looking for you."

"I am so glad. I guess I should ask how Lionel is? Do you know?"

"No, I haven't inquired as yet, nor have I inquired about my fellow officer that was injured. I came here first when I found out you had been installed back in your room."

"Would you like to see Lucinda? She hasn't finished feeding. I don't think, but I'm sure she won't mind."

The nurse helped her secure her gown before removing the blanket. The baby was making mewing sounds. Then Diana turned the baby for his viewing. Officer Jackson stepped closer to the bed.

"Mrs. Cardwell, she is so pretty. I mean that. Usually, I find newborns look like little old men but not this one. She is cute. I am glad you weren't badly injured and that you could be back with your baby. We can only be thankful a concerned citizen reported your husband's brutal act, or the story could have been a lot different. We may not have found you for days, as we had no idea of your destination."

"How is your partner?"

Officer Jackson offered, "I heard he might have rib problems and an injured leg. I should get down to see how he is coping. I just wanted to see you first. I like happy endings. I'm a sucker for babies." He put out his finger, trailing it gently across Lucinda's cheek. His smile increased as Lucinda's mouth searched for his finger.

"You better feed this young lady. She appears to be still hungry. I hope your arm isn't too painful?"

"It is throbbing, but my happiness of being with Lucinda is keeping the pain at bay. I don't want to take any medication for Lucinda's sake. I want to be able to nurse her myself. Thank you for rescuing me."

"You're welcome, even if it was a bit unorthodox way of doing it. Take care. I will be back to see you when I am in again." He didn't want to go into the details of the necessity of charging Lionel. Instead, he turned away to leave the room while Diana and Nurse Spiegel endeavored to help Lucinda return to her mother's breast. Lucinda had made attempts to cry while they were talking.

Officer Jackson went down to the Emergency to inquire about Mr. Cardwell and his partner Carl Thompson. He learned Lionel was in the OR, and Carl was getting strapped up in one of the side rooms. He went to the place the ER nurse indicated. The doctor had just stepped back, admiring his handiwork.

"Well, that should keep you a little more comfortable until those ribs heal. You were lucky that splintered one didn't pierce your lung. The other two ribs have cracks. Now we will take a look at the leg. Lie down." The doctor was helping him to lie down with the help of a nurse. The doctor stepped over to the X-ray setup on an illuminated viewer.

Jackson took the opportunity to speak to Carl. "Well, Carl, how do you feel?"

"Relieved that it wasn't more serious, Evan."

"Me too. I went to see Mrs. Cardwell first. She is back in her room in the hospital with her baby in her arms, feeding her. She has her left arm in a cast and contusions on her face. But I just found out that they were caused by Cardwell's ring when he was backhanding her face because she wanted to go back to her baby. Mother and baby looked delighted to be reunited."

"I am glad. I would hate to have the mother's death on my conscience. That thought went through my mind when I realized we were going to collide. How is Cardwell?"

"I don't know yet. Lionel is in the OR at the moment. How are you?"

"Thankful to be alive. It hurts to talk, but my leg doesn't feel too bad now."

The doctor approached the gurney. "The leg is nothing major, mostly bruising and muscle damage—no evidence of any broken bones. You're going to be limping for a while. I will prescribe some painkillers for those ribs. You are to take it easy for a while. When you play bumper cars, this is the result," The doctor expressed cheerfully.

"Thanks, Doc. I am glad I got off so lightly. The airbag saved me. Evan, how did you manage to get away without a scratch?" Everyone turned to Officer Jackson, sizing him up and down.

"Just lucky, I guess. The airbag certainly helped. The accident was a shock to my system. I am sure reaction will set in when I get away from here." He didn't bother mentioning that Lionel's airbag didn't deploy.

The doctor turned back to Carl. "Looks like your fellow officer has a lucky charm hidden somewhere. However, you will be in quite a bit of pain for a while. So, go home. Rest is required for a few days until those ribs heal. The cracked ones won't give you any problems. Are you taking him home?" he asked Evan.

"Yes, if I can round up a car. The one we were riding in didn't fare too well. But I will see this big lug gets settled in his bed."

"Okay, you can leave as soon as you get dressed." The doctor was busily writing on a pad. Finally, he ripped a sheet off and handed it to Carl. "A prescription for painkillers. You are going to need them, I'm afraid."

"Thanks again, Doc," said Carl as the doctor and nurse exited the room. Evan helped him dress to save him pain.

"While we are waiting for the car. I will check on Mr. Cardwell." He helped Carl walk out of the room. Carl was limping badly and doubled over a bit with the pain in his ribs. The nurse appeared with a wheelchair, which he was thankful to use.

"I guess I had better rent a cane when I go to pick up my painkillers. It sure is painful to walk."

Evan took over, pushing the wheelchair. So, the nurse could return to the busy emergency room. Other patients needed her attention.

"Let's go find out how Mr. Perfect is making out," said Carl facetiously.

When they inquired, the nurse said he was still in the OR. She didn't have any details as yet.

Evan asked Carl, "do you want to wait around if we can scrounge up a ride? I could always come back."

Carl replied, "I am in no hurry. I want to find out how Mr. Perfect makes out."

"How about the painkillers? You need to pick them up on the way home."

"As long as I am just sitting, the pain is bearable. I need to know about Lionel."

"Okay, we will wait, but I will still check in about a squad car for transport. First, let's find a phone. I am surprised Kelly hasn't been paging me by now."

"Yeah," chuckled Thompson, "the way I abolished the cruiser certainly warrants a frantic call from him. He takes every bump and nick personally. You would think he pays for the repairs out of his own pocket. But I guess when you work on these cars all the time, you must form an attachment of some kind. I think they become his babies somehow. Sometimes, I want to tell him to get a life."

"Kelly does seem to have quite a touch at keeping some of the older vehicles humming and roadworthy. I feel more confident in high-speed chases, knowing his skill has kept them in excellent shape, don't you?" Evan replied.

"Yes, I guess it is my warped sense of humor that likes to ride him. I should call my wife. If she hears about the accident on the news, she will worry."

"You can try my cell phone, but being inside this building might not give clear reception." Handing Carl his cell phone.

Carl quickly punched in her number. She answered after the second ring. Carl wanted to breeze over his injuries until he could be there with her. "Hi, love. I just want to let you know I will probably be home in an hour."

"Carl, are you okay? Did something happen? I haven't been listening to the news." The line started to crackle and break up. "Carl, are you still there? Are you all right?" Bonita was almost yelling.

"Yeah, Bonbon, I am all right. I just banged up the squad car a bit. My ribs and leg took the jolt. So, the doctor wants me to take it easy for a few days. But I will be home soon." He didn't know if she heard the last because the line had gone dead after much crackling.

He handed the cell phone back to Evan.

"Thanks, she wasn't listening to the news. So, I didn't need to call. So now she will worry until I get home. Damned if I do and damned if I don't call. But Bonita is a worrier. It is a relief when the kids do something, so she aims her worrying in that direction."

"Thank heavens Mary is more relaxed about the job than Bonita. She hardly misses a beat when I tell her about cases. Maybe she keeps it all stored up inside. I must ask her sometime. But I think I am chicken and try to keep the dangers of the job at bay. Let's find a nurse to see if Mr. Cardwell's out of the OR."

"We may locate a phone on the way to call the station. There is a nurse," pushing the wheelchair in that direction, but the nurse hurried into another room.

"We missed her. You wait here until she comes out. I will find a phone. I want a clear line when I talk to Captain Wilson. He hates cell phones and their reception problems."

Officer Jackson walked away after placing Carl safely away from the busy emergency room's hurrying traffic.

Evan asked a passing nurse, "can I use your phone at the information desk?"

She complied, "dial nine for an outside line."

Chapter Five

Diana had finished breastfeeding Lucinda when Dr. Sawyer appeared.

"Diana, are you all right? Look at you, what happened?"

She grinned at him. "I survived a crazy car ride with a crazy man. I am not letting it get me down. I am so happy to be back with Lucinda." She tightened her arms around her baby, who was sleeping peacefully. Nurse Spiegel had wanted to put Lucinda in her bassinet, but Diana had needed to hold onto her a while longer.

Nurse Spiegel looked on with interest, seeing that Diana wasn't becoming too exhausted after her experience.

"Well, you do look quite the picture with your arm in a cast and your face battered and bruised. Are you in much pain?" he took her hand, testing her pulse, which was racing.

"A little, but I want to feed my baby, so I don't want to take any medication." Her voice was almost reverent. Was it the relevance of feeding her baby and the closeness of the baby in her arms? Or was it Dr. Sawyer's fingers that were tracing the cuts and bruises on her face? His eyes were looking deeply into her eyes.

"Diana, these cuts are unusual to be from a car accident. What happened?" he asked quietly.

"Lionel didn't like the way I talked about going back for my baby. He had tied my hands behind me so that I couldn't get out of the car. I think that was why my arm got broken. Because I shouldn't have been in that position when the airbag exploded." Her voice was almost a whisper. Diana was nearly mesmerized by the way his fingers traced the cuts ever so lightly.

"The cuts, Diana? That doesn't explain the cuts."

"Lionel backhanded me. His ring was the cause of the cuts," Diana's voice faded.

Nurse Spiegel was as mesmerized as Diana. She expected to see Dr. Sawyer bend over to kiss the cuts better. This scene was playing out before her eyes was so intimate. She felt tingly as she slipped from the room.

"Diana, they are so deep," his voice was catching like he was feeling the cuts penetrating her delicate skin.

"Lionel has this raised square ring with an odd sign on it. He has worn it for years, even before I knew him. Lionel never takes it off. But he never talks about it either," Diana said ever so slowly. Her brown eyes were held by his blue eyes that were getting darker at his inner anger against Lionel.

The doctor leaned down. Diana knew that he was going to kiss the cuts better. Her hold on the baby must've tightened in anticipation. Lucinda let out a cry. Dr. Sawyer quickly straightened.

"Let me see this little lady?" Gently taking Lucinda out of her arms. He gazed down at her sweet face. "Hi, wee darling. You have your mommy back. You are a fortunate girl. Your mommy loves you very much." His eyes flipped back and forth from Diana to Lucinda as he talked. He kissed the baby's cheek as his eyes swung back to Diana. Dr. Sawyer recalled that she had an incredibly deep cut at the spot he kissed on Lucinda. The baby made a mewing sound.

"Well, little lady, you want your mommy, don't you? I don't blame you. She is a pretty special lady."

Diana raised her right arm to receive her baby, drawing her against her in a possessive way. "Doctor, do you know how Lionel is?" The air in the room changed, like the falling of day into night. Dr. Sawyer's shoulders stiffened. Gone was the intimacy if it was ever there.

"No. The only thing I have heard was Lionel was in the OR for a considerable time, but no details. I was anxious for you.

You didn't deserve your injuries. Also, I guarantee that Lucinda will be okay in time. Please believe me."

"I do. I've had faith in what you have said from the beginning. It was Lionel that wouldn't accept her the way she is with her legs."

"That is good to hear. Remember that, as Lucinda is growing stronger. No matter what, I will be there for Lucinda with the best possible attention. I am looking on the positive side. She may overcome the problem as her bones get stronger. We will put our trust in God and the future."

"Thank you, doctor. Yes, we will put our trust in God." Then she added, "no matter what happened to Lionel, I intend to leave him. I can't live with him ever again," she said shyly.

Where would she go? Where would they accept a mother and her baby who has no money? Maybe she was ridiculous. Her face saddened.

"Diana, I have a place for you and Lucinda to live. You will do light housekeeping only until your arm gets better and ready to go back to work full time. It is with my sister, Lucy. Her husband and son died recently. She is finding the house too empty without someone there. You would be helping her as much as you would be helping yourself. Your baby will be a boon to Lucy, helping her get over the loss of Connor. That was her son's name. He was five."

"Won't the baby be more of a reminder?"

"The age variance will make all the difference. Lucy wants you there. I know it will work. Now, I have to get back to my patients. I think you should try to sleep while Lucinda is sleeping if you can. I will send Nurse Spiegel back in. Although, you probably don't need a personal nurse anymore. But she will be with you for one more day, at least."

"Dr. Sawyer, will you let me know about Lionel? I don't intend to live with him ever again. I just need to know about his condition. Thank you for arranging things with your sister. But I doubt I will be much help to her with my arm in a cast."

"You will get used to it and compensate in no time. Besides, it's the company Lucy wants as much as the housekeeping." He paused, then added. "I will get the details on Lionel for you."

Diana's eyes followed him out of the room. How could she feel that way towards him? Was she reading more into his actions than possibly were there? She had heard stories of patients falling in love with their doctors. Was that what was happening to her? Was she interpreting too much into his kindness?

Her thoughts should be on Lionel. But, no, Lionel destroyed that when he kidnapped me and denied their baby's existence to his parents. She would never forgive him for that.

Nurse Spiegel breezed into the room, saying, "it is nappy time. Pass me that bundle of joy. You try to close your eyes and rest." She whisked the baby away before Diana had a chance to complain.

Maybe she should try to rest while she had an opportunity. Her mind was still in a dither over Dr. Sawyer. However, the pain of her injuries was slowly coming to the foreground. If she could sleep, maybe the pain would recede again. She closed her eyes.

It was kind of Dr. Sawyer to ask his sister to take Lucinda and her in. Would he come around to see them? No, get that thought out of your head right now, she ordered. Dr. Sawyer is a very nice man. That is all there is to his kindness. Her tired body was slowly slipping into sleep.

Nurse Spiegel had been watching her intently, wondering about the play of emotions on her delicate face. Did anything happen between them while she was out of the room? Diana did not wear the look of a kissed woman when she breezed back in. Maybe she was mistaken at the intimacy of Dr. Sawyer's fingers on Diana's face. Perhaps he was trying to calm her, feeling terrible for the unkind reason for her facial injuries. Dr. Sawyer was a very caring man towards his patients. Besides, Diana wasn't his patient, but she felt that Dr. Sawyer treated her that way. Yes, that is all it is. He is a caring doctor for all patients. She scolded herself. After all, Mrs. Cardwell had been through a lot today.

Nurse Spiegel's hand went out to pat the sleeping baby. "You are a lucky girl to have a mommy love you the way your mother does," she murmured.

**

Officer Jackson wandered back to find Carl. "Well, buddy, did you find out anything yet?"

Carl's head whipped around at his partner's voice. "No, but I can tell you the pain of these ribs is driving me crazy. So, I was going to ask for a painkiller before I ask about Mr. Cardwell."

"The car will be here soon. Then we will get you fixed up. In the meantime, we'll see what we can find out about Mr. Cardwell."

The nurse they had previously been talking to flitted their way.

"Nurse, where can we find out how Mr. Cardwell is doing?"

"Officer, if you check with Recovery, he may be there by now. He was pretty bad when he came in, I understand. Follow the blue line. It will take you there from here."

Evan was pushing Carl in the wheelchair. He looked at the several colored lines painted on the floor, following the blue line.

They saw the sign at the same time. A nurse was proceeding into the room in their path.

"Nurse, can you tell me how Mr. Cardwell is doing?"

"No, he never showed up here yet. Perhaps he is still in OR."

"Can you check for me?"

Another nurse was bustling by, with her hair covered with a paper covering. A mask hung around her neck.

"This nurse may be able to tell you. She works in OR." Her hand waved in the bustling nurse's direction.

Officer Jackson headed for her, hoping to cut her off. "Nurse, can you tell me anything about Mr. Cardwell?"

"Cardwell, he must be the man who is still in OR. They are trying to save his badly crushed legs. He should be out soon. I doubt he will ever walk again. If he does, it will probably be with only one leg."

Evan and Carl exchanged glances.

"Thank you, nurse." Unfortunately, she had already rushed away.

Carl smiled. "Yes, Mr. Perfect isn't perfect anymore. His legs crushed, isn't that ironic, Evan?"

"Yes, I never thought I would feel like that about another person's mishap. But on this guy, it seems poetic justice." Evan smiled. "Let's go, buddy. Your chariot awaits, I am sure."

"Okay, I need some painkillers. These ribs are a bummer the way they are hurting." Carl still wore a secret grin of satisfaction at Lionel's dilemma. Evan directed the wheelchair out of the entrance to await the police cruiser.

**

The patient wheeled out of the OR was still unconscious. Upon awakening, he will find that as much as the Orthopedic doctor had tried, he had not been able to save his left leg. His right leg would leave him with a limp even if they fitted his left leg with a prosthetics. But that was down the road after the stump had healed. The doctors had removed his left leg at the knee.

Mr. Cardwell's destination was the recovery room. He was fortunate that his other injuries were minor cuts and bruises. However, he would be a while getting mobile again.

At the door of the Recovery room, the gurney was taken by another nurse for placement. The nurse busied herself taking his vital signs. She would attend to him until he recovered from the anesthetic. It was a while before the nurse was able to bring him back to awareness. But when he had recovered enough to answer her, she started walking away.

"Nurse, why are my legs covered this way? What happened to them?"

"Mr. Cardwell, you have your left leg amputated at the knee, and your right leg was saved but was badly injured too. The doctors did everything they could to save them both."

"That can't be," he said in a strained voice. "I can feel the pain in both of my lower legs."

"Yes, Mr. Cardwell, people say that after they have their leg removed. They say they can still feel their toes are itchy or sore. But I have to tell you that it isn't possible because your lower left leg is gone. I'm sorry."

Lionel let out a shriek that was sharply curtailed by his dry throat.

"This cannot be. I have to have my legs. I run every day to keep fit. I need my legs." His eyes filled with tears as he started to snivel and cry openly.

Now that he was out of the anesthetic, the nurse could give him a sedative until he came out of his grief. It would be best to keep him out for a while. The nurse hung a bag to the pole. Then she arranged the transport of the patient to his hospital room. Mr. Cardwell was not going to adjust quickly to his fate. She could tell from the way he was reacting. She didn't envy the nurses who would have to look after him on Three West.

Sometimes you can tell a problem patient as soon as they recover from the anesthetic. This one, she felt, was one of them. She wiped his face and crooned to him, trying to calm him until the medication kicked in. She didn't want him to pull out the needle in his agitation.

Some days it was hard to witness the people in trauma that passed through here daily. But as a nurse, she enjoyed her position in Recovery. So, she had to keep her emotions under control.

Mr. Cardwell seemed to be settling down at last as the orderlies arrived to transport him to Three West.

The nurse looked to the door where another patient was arriving that would need her attention. She walked in that direction to receive the new patient. Life goes on, and her shift was almost over.

**

It was late evening when Dr. Sawyer dropped by to see if Diana was awake. All was peaceful and quiet. Diana and the baby in the bassinet beside the bed were sleeping. Diana must have heard him because her eyelids fluttered then opened.

He came over to her. "Diana, did I wake you? I tried to be quiet."

"No, I just put the baby down. I wasn't fully asleep yet. I was wondering about Lionel. No one has said anything to me."

"That is why I am here. Lionel didn't fare too well. They had to amputate his lower left leg, and his right leg is injured too. He will probably walk with a limp on the right leg and have an artificial left leg."

Dr. Sawyer kept his expression bland. He didn't want to show his feelings in the matter one way or the other for Diana's sake.

"Oh, no. That is terrible. Lionel certainly won't accept that easily. He is a runner. He insists on running every day, rain or shine. He certainly won't like that."

"Diana, I have to ask. Are you still wanting a place to stay for you in your baby?"

She paused then looked him in the eyes. "Do you think it is cruel of me to want to be away from Lionel?"

"Good heavens, no."

"I cannot continue with my marriage to a man that would even consider denying the birth of his child. I can't forgive him for that ever. I am sorry about his legs, but I still want to be away from him. Do you think I am unkind?" Diana timidly asked.

"Any man who denies a baby like Lucinda doesn't deserve her. So no, I don't think you are unkind. Lucy, my sister, will be happy to hear that you are coming. I will call her first thing tomorrow. She may call me tonight if she has trouble sleeping, which she quite often does. She knows I am home late Wednesday nights. She will be anxious to hear your decision," he smiled winningly at her. Deep down, he knew his inner feelings were being affected by this woman.

"I hope your sister likes Lucinda and me. Lucinda seems to be a good baby, as long as I feed her," Diana said hopefully.

"Don't worry about that. Lucy loves babies. She knows they have crying spells. After all, she had Connor, you know."

"I was afraid after my accident that I wouldn't be able to feed Lucinda. But she is settling in quite nicely." Why was she so shy with Dr. Sawyer? Was she reading more into his manner than he was giving? She had only met Dr. Sawyer a few days ago. It must be her hormones out of control, having just had a baby. She had read something about raging hormones after birth. I hope that is all it is. I don't want to embarrass Dr. Sawyer if I live at his sister's home. I will be seeing him socially, no doubt.

Dr. Sawyer thought that her long period of quietness meant that she wanted to sleep. He had assured her that the baby was doing fine on her breast milk. She didn't reply. He was reluctant to leave, enjoying looking at her. Her big brown eyes were so bright.

"I'd better let you get some sleep. It has been a very long day for you. Is your arm bothering you?" He hated the evidence of Lionel's ring maiming her face.

"It is throbbing. But I am mostly being hampered by the cast when I shift Lucinda around. That bothers me more."

Dr. Sawyer's fingers went out against his will, touching her face ever so gently.

"I hate to see your face marred this way. I want to say your husband deserves his injuries, but as a doctor, I wouldn't wish them on anyone. Now, he is worse off than Lucinda will ever be." His fingers were roaming her face.

Diana's face was tingling but not in pain but excitement of those wandering fingertips. Lucinda gave a little cry. His hand dropped away.

"She must have a bit of gas." Dr. Sawyer said as he walked over to the bassinet. He picked up Lucinda, lifting her to his shoulder. He gently patted her back. Lucinda gave a delicate burp. "That's my girl," he said triumphantly, then laid her down again.

Those big brown eyes filled with love as she looked at her baby. Diana was amazed that she didn't mind him touching Lucinda. It had made her flutter inside to see him hugging her baby so naturally. Was he married? Did he have children? She hadn't thought of him as being married before. Her raging hormones were certainly active.

"Goodnight, Diana."

"Goodnight, Dr. Sawyer."

He crossed the floor then waved from the door as she shut the light off. She lay there thinking back on all that had happened during the day. She cradled her arm, wishing the throbbing would recede.

She had been so fearful she would never see her baby again. Lionel had been so forceful. She couldn't fight him. But the scary part was when the police were chasing them. She kept yelling for him to stop. But Lionel had shouted back at her to keep quiet, delivering another backhand to her face.

She was too afraid after that to do anything. When Diana saw the truck start to pull out in front of them, she had thought they were going to die for sure. But, as much as her arm was throbbing, she felt she had gotten off relatively lightly, considering crashing first into the truck, and then the police cruiser hitting them. Thankfully the airbag helped with that.

Imagine Lionel having his leg amputated and his other leg injured. Now, who was the gimp Diana wanted to ask him?

Was she wrong to leave him under these circumstances? No! She remembered the shock on Lionel's parent's faces when they realized the baby was alive. How cruel it was of Lionel to tell them that the baby had died. Impossible after that for her to stay with him after he intended to abandon his baby.

While Lionel was in the hospital, she would move the baby's things and hers to Lucy's place. Before Lionel was injured, she had thought she would have to give up everything, knowing he would not let her have anything of hers or the baby's if she intended to leave him. He would have been vindictive that way.

Diana knew she would have to depend on Dr. Sawyer to retrieve her things from the house. She didn't want to ever go inside that house again. The memory of Lionel hitting her and yelling would always be with her whenever she thought of him. Diana just hoped the welts on her face wouldn't leave noticeable scars. Oh well, get over the self-pity.

She was looking forward to starting a new life for herself and her baby. She hoped that Lucy was as pleasant as Dr. Sawyer. Then she would know she was doing the right thing.

Diana felt Dr. Sawyer's fingers caress her battered face as she slipped into sleep. She smiled.

Chapter Six

Dr. Sawyer arrived with Dr. McIntyre.

"Well, you have had quite a time since your delivery. I'm sorry your husband was unable to accept Dr. Sawyer's views on your daughter's legs. My! My! You do look a little worse for wear, my dear. Dr. Sawyer filled me in on your kidnapping and your injuries. You don't look well enough to be released, but Dr. Sawyer has promised to take good care of you and your baby. So, I am going to arrange for your release into his care. How is that, my dear?"

"Do you really mean it? I can leave today?"

"I don't see why not as long as Dr. Sawyer is taking responsibility for you. After all, Troy is a doctor. Diana, did you know Dr. Sawyer's name is Troy?"

Diana looked at Dr. Sawyer then slid back to Dr. McIntyre. "No, I didn't, but I think I like that name. But I will call him Dr. Sawyer for now."

"As you wish. I will go and sign the form for your release so that you can get dressed. I will arrange to have a nurse come to help you. Come along, Troy. The young lady wants to get dressed."

Dr. Sawyer chuckled. "Yes, doctor. I don't think Diana would take too kindly to my playing nursemaid while she dresses."

The two doctors trooped out of the room. A nurse arrived shortly after.

"I hear you are being released today. Let me help you get dressed. Then we will see to the baby." The nurse went to the locker to remove Diana's clothes, bringing them over to the bed. Diana was already standing beside the bed, waiting to be helped. After which, the nurse dressed Lucinda with care and a lot of cooing.

Diana looked on with a smile at her daughter's acceptance of the nurse's cooing. It touched her heart that Lucinda was hers. The wonderment of having the responsibility for this young life. The miracle of birth was just sinking in. She was ready to go when Dr. Sawyer arrived back with a wheelchair.

"Your chariot awaits, my lady," he said gallantly.

The nurse placed the baby in her arms after she was seated. Diana thanked her for her help.

"Home, my lord," Diana said with a giggle.

The nurse's laughter joined Dr. Sawyer's at Diana's come back. They were a cheerful couple as they made their way through the halls. Eventually, Dr. Sawyer had them both installed in the front seat of his Mercedes.

"I don't have a car seat or carrier for the baby. I should have thought ahead about that. But I didn't expect you to be released today. So, I came unprepared. Sorry. We will stop on the way to pick up some things for the baby."

"If you take me home, I have all we need for Lucinda there. Is it possible to arrange to have Lucinda's furnishings and apparel delivered to your sister's place? If she has room, that is?"

"Lucy was wondering about the baby's things. She is prepared to outfit her for you. But now that won't be necessary. Lionel's lengthy stay in the hospital will curtail him from stopping you. Where do you live?"

"I live in the suburb of Nelson. You reach it by going via Emerson Street to Detroit Avenue. Once you reach the development, we are on the first street left off of Emerson. The house has a blue door, 1510 Temple St. Do you know where Emerson is?"

"Yes, I am familiar with that area. Lucy is not too far from there. So, it will be no problem to find." The Mercedes cruised the streets with ease, lapping up the miles until the turnoff.

Diana's stomach clenched at her last memories of being here. They weren't so pleasant. She must have grasped Lucinda too tightly because Lucinda gave out a little cry. "I am sorry baby. I didn't mean to squeeze you," she said regretfully.

Dr. Sawyer looked over at her after he pulled into the driveway. "Diana, you will only have to be here long enough to show me what needs moving. Then we will leave. I understand how you feel being here. You sit here while I come around to take Lucinda and help you out." Opening the door, he quickly eased from the car. Then he circled in front of the vehicle to Diana's door. Opening it, Dr. Sawyer reached for the baby. Then he took Diana's arm to help her from the car.

She was a bit awkward with her left arm in a cast. But she managed with Dr. Sawyer's help as gracefully as possible. He took the key from Diana to open the door which was already unlocked. From her story, he was not surprised that it was already open in Lionel's haste to leave the premises. She entered with some trepidation. Dr. Sawyer suggested they go directly to the baby's room.

He was impressed with the décor of the room. It had storybook characters dancing across the walls in a parade of pastels with highlights in dark colors as accents. The furniture was white, letting the walls warm the room, and bring the room to life.

Unfortunately, Lionel's rage of devastation in the room was unpleasant. She knew Dr. Sawyer was trying to ignore the situation by commenting, "Did you do the decorating?

Diana surveyed the room, trying to be upbeat. "I did. I purchased some nursery rhyme books. It took me weeks before I finished. I wanted the room to be a labor of love for my baby."

"Diana, it certainly is that. It is a shame Lucinda will not get the benefit of this. When I come to help arrange the removal of these things, I will bring a camera. I will take pictures for you to show Lucinda later on in life." While he was talking, he was tidying the room's mess. "Can I get a box or bags to pack some of the baby's immediate necessities?" He laid Lucinda down in her crib that he had straightened.

"Yes, there are boxes or bags down in the pantry off the kitchen. I will start to put together some things while you find them."

Diana started packing the diaper bag with baby powder, oil, and diapers. She placed little undershirts, nighties, sweaters, and bonnet sets on the changing table. Her heart tightened at the way Lionel had destroyed the room. Diana felt the need to escape, so she controlled her feelings with some difficulty.

She concentrated on picking out a bottle brush, baby bottles, nipples to be used for water and juice in between feedings. She laid out quite a few things, such as bedding and clothes. She wasn't quite sure how much he intended to take right now.

Dr. Sawyer arrived back with a box and a couple of shopping bags.

"I dropped off some shopping bags in your bedroom so you can pack some of your clothes too. If you take care of your personal items, I will bring the rest of your clothes later. You can make a list as to where I can find things, or you can come back with me while Lucy watches the baby." He gave her a choice as he could see that she was finding it difficult to be here.

"I think I will give you a list. I don't want to come back here ever again." Diana looked around Lucinda's room with some regret. The hours it had taken to make this room unique to give her baby happy hours. However, Lionel's devastation of one of the walls spoilt it for her.

"Diana, I'll pack these. You go to your bedroom. Pack your things quickly, and we will get out of here as soon as possible."

She walked down the hall. Upon entering the bedroom, the first thing she noticed was the pile of discarded blankets Lionel had wrapped her in when he kidnapped her from the hospital. Her heart thudded against her ribs. She started to cry. Why had Lionel acted that way? He had behaved like a madman. She grabbed the shopping bags and headed to the dresser. She started throwing in underclothes and nighties helter-skelter. Then she went to the closet and threw in shoes and a couple of changes of clothes, not packing too carefully as the tears streamed down her face. She left the room as fast as possible, carrying the lightest bag in her left hand.

She met Dr. Sawyer, leaving the baby's room with the box and bags. He set them down as he saw Diana's face wet with tears. He drew her into his arms, bags and all. He let her cry against his chest. "Diana, let's get out of here. You never have to come back." The emotion in his voice was of great tenderness.

"Lucinda is still sleeping. So, let's get these things out to the car. Then I will come back to get her. I will put her in the car carrier." Diana managed to straighten up. She wiped her tears on the handkerchief that Dr. Sawyer handed her. It was challenging to use the handkerchief because she still retained the shopping bags' handles in each hand.

They headed out the front door without looking back. Troy packed the car but left room for the baby carrier, which he intended to strap into the back seat.

Diana continued wiping her eyes with the hanky, as the tears insisted on falling even though she had left the house. She finally was able to control the waterworks as she saw Dr. Sawyer returning with the baby carrier. There appeared to be no movement from the baby as Dr. Sawyer quickly carried her to the car across the lawn. Lucinda must still be sleeping.

He opened the back door. The baby carrier fitted into the roomy rear seat, belting it in securely. As he slipped into the car behind the wheel, he said, "let's go meet Lucy. She will be waiting for you both. She sounded quite excited when I called her to say you were coming today."

The powerful car covered the miles to Lucy's place. When they pulled up in front, a young woman ran towards the car. Lucy must have been waiting in the front window for the silver car's appearance.

The car barely stopped when Lucy whipped open the car door. "Hi, everyone," she said gaily, "I saw you as soon as you turned the corner. Am I anxious or what?" Troy joined in his sister's laughter.

"Diana, I would like you to meet my sister, Lucy. Lucy, this is Diana, and the squirming baby in the back is Lucinda."

When Diana removed herself from the car with Lucy's help, she looked in the back seat. Lucinda was indeed squirming, making quiet crying sounds that were steadily getting louder.

"Oh, no. I guess Lucinda is hungry. I am sorry you will be greeting her while she is in a full-blown crying jag."

Lucy said, "don't worry about it. Babies will cry if they are wet and hungry. Let's get her inside quickly. So, you can attend to her. I placed a rocker in the baby's room that will be perfect for feeding her. The room is pretty bare until Troy brings the baby's furniture. I removed my son's things when I heard you were coming for sure. I should have removed them long ago, but somehow, I couldn't bring myself to do it. It all seemed so final if I did. But with your coming with Lucinda, it didn't seem so bad after all." she said in a lilting voice.

Troy was laughing. "Just call Lucy, motor mouth. She is inclined to run over with enthusiasm when she gets an audience."

He had removed the baby carrier from the back seat.

"Give her to me. I want to see my new charge." Lucy took the handle of the carrier out of Troy's hand. Lucinda had calmed down a bit with the movement of the carrier.

"You are a wee darling. Oh, Troy, she is beautiful. Diana, she is beautiful."

Diana was smiling. She instantly liked this exuberant woman even though she was tall and quite full-figured and dwarfed Diana.

Diana and Lucinda responded enjoyably to Lucy's spontaneous welcome. Lucy kept dragging Troy playfully into the midst of every conversation.

Diana noticed the closeness of their relationship. The intertwining of their thoughts and actions. It was a new experience for her. Being an only child raised by mature parents, she became an adult before her time.

Troy showed Diana their rooms. "Make yourself comfortable. So, you can feed Lucinda with ease." Diana excused herself to go to the washroom.

Troy went back to the kitchen.

"Well, sis, what do you think?" his voice held a shimmer of excitement.

Lucy had the baby freshly diapered. "Troy, this is going to be so wonderful. I always wanted a sister, thanks for bringing Diana here. Lucinda is a beautiful little doll. How could any man reject her the way Diana's husband did?"

"I don't know either. Lucinda is a wee darling."

Lucy had the baby carrier on the kitchen table. Lucinda was unwrapped and kicking freely. The hovering of the brother and sister was holding her attention. She had temporarily forgotten her thirst for her mommy's milk.

Lucinda was unused to being unwrapped. She was trying to focus on these two tall beings, slightly bent over her, cooing their delight.

"Troy, this is going to be perfect. I am so glad Diana stuck with her decision to strike out on her own. I wondered after I heard her husband was seriously injured if she would change her mind."

"Yes, well, being kidnapped and forced to abandon her baby made the husband less than dear to her anymore." Troy broke off as Diana arrived back in the room. Lucinda was working into a fury in need of feeding. He did not want to make Diana uncomfortable, excusing himself to get the rest of Diana's things from the car.

As he followed the voices, Troy found Diana on the sofa with pillows supporting the baby and her encased arm. She had a baby cover over her shoulder, covering the view of her exposed breast. Diana's feet were on an ottoman, so she was completely relaxed.

Lucy was sitting beside her, perched on the edge of the sofa facing the feeding mother. Lucy's spontaneous nature had the two ladies talking happily. They were chatting like old friends already, which pleased Troy.

"Is everyone comfortable?" An entirely unnecessary comment with the scene before him. "Can I make some tea or coffee? How about lunch Lucy, is it planned?"

"Troy is always hungry. I only see him when he wants a meal, which is often." Lucy sent Troy a loving look. Their relaxed enjoyment of each other's company was evident.

"There is a casserole in the oven and salad made in the refrigerator. It will be ready when Diana finishes nursing Lucinda."

"Diana, do you want a drink? Ignore my sister. You must be thirsty by now. Juice, tea, coffee?"

"No, thank you, Dr. Sawyer. I'll wait for lunch."

"Troy. There is no Dr. Sawyer here. Call me, Troy." He quickly reiterated. "Well, I am thirsty, and I am going to have coffee. I will bring you juice, Diana. Lucy coffee or juice?"

"Juice will be fine for me too." Lucy sent him a winsome look as he exited the room.

"Diana, I want you to feel free to make this house your home. I want you to feel comfortable within these walls. This is your home now, yours and Lucinda's. You have no idea how much your presence is going to mean to me. I have been rattling around in this big house too long by myself. The house needs people, love, and laughter,"

Lucy's friendly voice of welcome made Diana relax. This homey house when Troy had shown her around made her feel comfortable immediately.

Lucinda's bow-shaped mouth was openly searching for her mother's nipple. The cast was a problem. Lucy helped Diana with the pillows as they adjusted Lucinda onto her other breast.

Troy stood watching his sister with a pleased expression. Lucy was oozing enjoyment of the opportunity to help with the baby and Diana. He knew she had mourned too long for her late husband and son. They had been killed in a car accident by a drunk driver.

Lucy had managed to get her business life back to normal. But her social life, he knew was almost nil. Other than their dinners together, he knew Lucy didn't participate too often in the night scene. Although her friends frequently asked her to join them.

This move was going to be so good for both of them. Troy felt great satisfaction as he placed a tray of drinks on the coffee table.

The conversation was free-flowing. No one seemed to notice the time passing. Diana felt blessed that these two people were to be part of her life. She realized Lucinda had dropped her nipple and had fallen asleep. She lifted Lucinda to her shoulder, patting her back. Lucy excused herself to get lunch on the table.

"Dr. Sawyer, I can't thank you enough for bringing me to your sister."

"The name is Troy. Dr. Sawyer is only usable in the hospital, and you are welcome. Lucy is so alive now that you both are here. It has been a long time since she has been this animated. I have noticed such a change already. So, I am thanking you. Now, do you feel comfortable enough to make this your home?"

"Dr. Saw. . . Troy, I do feel very comfortable. Lucy has made me feel very welcome. I know Lucinda will benefit from your sister's exuberance too. She loves babies, doesn't she?"

"Yes, she always wanted a brood, but for some reason, she only had Connor."

"I wanted more children too. But now it looks like Lucinda will be my only one."

"You are young yet, Diana. You might find someone that wants to have children with you." Troy didn't want to say that he would be willing. It was too soon.

Lucy came to the door.

"Lunch is ready in the kitchen. Come on, you two. Lucinda can be put in her carrier to slumber. She is sleeping quite comfortably in your arms, Diana. Help Diana up, Troy, be a gentleman." She teased easily.

Troy leaped over to Diana, taking the baby in one arm, lifting Diana with his other hand, following Lucy. Diana walked beside him, and Troy kept his hand casually on her back in a companionable way.

Lucy had placed the baby carrier near the table. Troy gently put the sleeping Lucinda down. They made a cozy family as they sat to eat the delicious meal.

Troy excused himself as soon as lunch was over. Teasing Lucy that she wouldn't expect him to take her out for dinner as often now since she had a new housemate.

Lucy replied, "big brother, you could always take us all out. Look how well Lucinda sleeps." She easily chided back.

"I am willing anytime. I will even be expecting some home-cooked meals."

Lucy hated to cook. She was hoping Diana would take over the cooking. But that wouldn't be until she was used to the cast, which was limiting.

Diana watched the brother and sister spar playfully. She had never experienced this kind of camaraderie before. Certainly not with Lionel. These two made her smile with enjoyment as Troy playfully hugged his sister, giving her a resounding smacking kiss on the cheek.

"Troy, you will have to improve on your kissing if you want to attract a girl," giving him a light poke.

"How about right now." He bent over to kiss Diana lingeringly. Diana could barely get her breath after he stood up. "Practice does improve the kiss, wouldn't you say? Bye, Sis. Bye, Diana." He sailed out the door as if nothing unusual had happened. Diana lightly ran the tips of her fingers over her kissed lips.

"Don't take any notice of him, Diana. He is all bluster. Shall we get the table cleared? Then we can get you settled in. Maybe you should catch a nap while Lucinda is sleeping."

Diana cleared with her right hand as best she could. "Yes, maybe, I will."

"I have some work I want to finish on my computer. So, I won't be requiring any attention for a while. We will work out your duties as your arm becomes less of a problem."

Lucy worked efficiently with a natural haste, as she seemed to do everything. Diana hoped that Lucy didn't expect more from her than she could give. She headed for her bedroom with Lucy trailing behind her with the sleeping baby in the carrier. Lucy slipped Lucinda into her new room.

When Diana awoke, she could hear Lucy singing in Lucinda's room. Diana surmised Lucinda was awake. Lucy was entertaining her. Diana glanced at the clock beside the bed. She was amazed to see she had slept for almost three hours. She seldom slept more than cat naps during the day.

The unexpected change in her life must've eased her mind and relaxed her. Lionel was a force that demanded her constant attention with his rigid control that kept her forever cleaning and straightening the already clean house. She realized now that she had worried that Lucinda's arrival in the home wouldn't give her the time to devote to the exact perfection that Lionel fully expected. Towels in alignment, color coordinated. The cans in the cupboard by size and rows. Cushions lying angle-wise rather than just thrown. His suits by colors in the closet and his drawers fully folded, in exact order.

Diana realized that this had been bothering her for a significant time. But she had decided she was going to devote proper time to Lucinda instead. That meant the house would no longer be a showplace of perfection.

To show her defiance, Diana straightened the covers but not too perfectly. Then she moved the bottles around in the bathroom, so they were haphazard in size. Diana left the towels a little out of kilter. She felt much better as she headed towards Lucy's voice and her daughter.

Lucy looked up as Diana entered. "Lucinda and I are becoming close friends. Aren't we, little one?" she looked down at Lucinda's little pink face. "Diana, she is so perfect. When I sing to her, I think she likes it."

"I can't believe I slept so long. Surely Lucinda needs feeding? I expected to wake up with her crying."

"Maybe, my voice mesmerized her. Because she has been just laying here watching me. Did you have a good sleep?"

"Yes, I never sleep like that during the day."

"Diana, you have been through rather a lot emotionally lately. So, I guess your body needed relaxation. How about we get you two settled for Lucinda's feeding. Then I will whip up some dinner. I have to confess. I am not much of a cook and never have been. Mark used to do the cooking in self-defense when he was alive. Oh, Diana, I miss him so and Connor too." Her voice changed to profound sadness.

"Lucy, I am so sorry you lost them. However, I can imagine how much of a loss you are feeling without them. I hardly had Lucinda with me, yet I was devastated when Lionel separated us. I was hysterical most of the time, needing Lucinda. Lionel wouldn't listen to me. In his mind, Lucinda had died. How could that be when Lucinda dropped into his hands at birth. It was supposed to have been a special bond for him. But when he learned she might have an imperfection, he closed her out of his life."

The wonderment of Lionel's weird way of thinking was very evident in Diana's explanation, plus a great deal of hurt.

"Well, it is his loss and my gain. I am going to love you both very much." Lucy had been settling Diana in the rocking chair, propping her arms with pillows while they were talking. Lucinda greedily suckled her mother's breast.

"Lucy, am I terrible because I am glad Lionel injured his legs during the car crash. After the way, he called his daughter a 'gimp.' That word hurt me so much at the time."

"No, Diana. It is perfectly normal to have those feelings under the circumstances. I, too, would have felt the same if I was in your position."

"But, Lucy, I didn't even express concern when I heard he lost his left leg at the knee and injured the right one, which would leave him with a limp."

"Diana, he hurt you too deeply by rejecting Lucinda. So, it is quite normal for you to react the way you do." She avoided saying anything about Diana's face, which Troy had mentioned privately about Lionel's backhanding her during the kidnapping.

"Now, let's get dinner started. The subject of Lionel is taboo for the rest of the day." Lucy left the room with a new buoyancy to her walk, now that the house had new voices in it. She felt that Diana and Lucinda would help fill the empty void left by Mark and Connor's passing.

Chapter Seven

As the days went by, Diana became more carefree and cheerful under Lucy's guidance. Every day was like a blessing in this joyful household. Diana had not felt this relaxed since she married Lionel five years ago.

It now penetrated her mind that the persnickety manner required to organize the house for Lionel's approval had unknowingly put a strain on her for such a long time because of its consequences. There was seldom laughter or smiling in their daily lives.

Diana felt that she had shed ten years. She felt younger, which inspired her to sing to the baby. She and Lucy occasionally sang duets. Laughter was a big part of their day, giving her a feeling of belonging in a caring home atmosphere.

She was mastering some of the difficulties hindered by the cast on her left arm. She was compensating to a degree so that she was more self-sufficient with the baby and the housework. She insisted on helping with her keep. Cooking was her territory now, with a bit of help from Lucy.

Lucy insisted on helping with Lucinda, such as bathing and changing her. Lucy enjoyed this immensely. Diana couldn't do it with her cast. So, it worked out well for both of them.

Lucy's business was going well now that she was happier. It was no longer a chore, as it had been in her loneliness.

Troy showed up frequently, breezing in and out of their lives, playing the poor bachelor that needed a homecooked meal for his survival.

Diana wondered why Troy wasn't married. She soon found out he had not found the girl of his dreams mainly because being a doctor was his concentration. Lucy was generous with information about her childhood and the closeness of their family life. Troy and his parents showed up occasionally for dinner. Diana felt overwhelmed the first time they came with their families' high spirits and laughter. It was a new experience in her solemn life.

Lucy's parents made a fuss of Lucinda like it was their grandchild. Lucinda was turning into quite the charmer. Cooing and blowing bubbles to the delight of everyone. Diana's heart burst with feelings of belonging, looking at the delightful people with their caring attitude towards her and the baby.

They were teasing her that she would miss her trusty cast as it had been eight weeks. She laughed at their teasing. Diana was adamant that she could give up the cast without any attachment to it. Tomorrow she was going back to the hospital to have it removed. The plan was for Troy to take her to the hospital while Lucy minded Lucinda. Troy offered to pick Diana up at 10:00 AM the following day.

Goodbyes said all around as the evening ended. Lucy and Diana waved to the departing parents and Troy.

While they were tidying up, Lucy said, "Diana, I want you to know how much having you here has added to my life. My parents have noticed such a difference in me. They were commenting on it while you were in the kitchen with Troy, preparing the dessert. You are so easy to talk to and be with. I think of you more like a sister."

"It has been wonderful being here. You have no idea the life I led until I came here. My parent's opinion was that a child was seen but not heard. I was an adult at six, with the result that I had few friends in my school days. I met Lionel through some of my father's business associates. My parents encouraged the relationship so much that I was married before I had time to think."

"What happened?" asked Lucy with interest.

"There was an arranged wedding between Lionel's parents and mine. Probably Lionel was in on some of it. I was never consulted or even asked by Lionel for my hand in marriage. All I knew was that the parents were arranging a party. I thought it was an engagement party. To my horror, when I arrived at the party with my parents, there was a minister. The vows were said. I must have repeated the necessary words in my numbed state because there was a ring on my finger. Everyone was saying congratulations. All the guests were business people connected to my parents and some of Lionel's parents' friends and family."

"There was no honeymoon. Lionel couldn't take time off work. He was significantly older than I. Lionel had saved his money, so he had bought a house. It was not a cheerful house. I had changed one drab life for another."

Lucy was amazed at the story that Diana was telling of her life. Diana continued.

"But Lionel did seem more excitable and affectionate to me at the thought of the baby. I thought I was going to have a more loving existence. He felt exalted when Lucinda dropped into his hands. He was openly affectionate to me for the wonder of our baby. But as you know, this soon changed upon Troy's evaluation of her legs."

"Oh, dear," Lucy sympathized.

"Lionel became impossible after hearing the news of some potential problem with Lucinda's legs. He is such a meticulous man requiring his clothes hung by type and color. His drawers were neat to perfection. Towels had to be hung just so and cans in a row by size in the cupboard and the fridge in an established pattern. Lionel was Mr. Perfection. To find out Lucinda might have a defect in her legs was beyond him." Her voice trailed off.

"Oh, Diana, that is so sad. It was just the opposite of my life, so full of friends and loving parents. My husband was Sir Galahad that came to my rescue in my late teens. I was trail riding on a horse that was spooked, causing it to flee in terror. I was clinging for dear life. Mark appeared out of nowhere, sitting upon a powerful black horse. The horse ate up the distance between us and saved me just as my horse raced towards a high fence. I knew if he jumped it, that would be the end of me. But Mark grabbed the bridal and calmed the horse down."

"I think I fell in love with him at that moment. But it was a year before we were married. Every moment was heaven after that. Mark was such fun to live with, caring, funny, and very loving. When we had Connor a year later, he was so happy and proud. Conner was like his father. Our life together as a family was wonderful until that drunk snuffed out their lives and turned me into a grieving widow. I wanted to die too."

"That must have been so sad for you. I don't know how you survived it. The thought of not seeing Lucinda ever again was devastating for me."

"Now, with you and Lucinda here, I can look back at all of our good times and feel warm all over. We lived life to the fullest every day of our marriage. You have given me a new life and a new chance at loving and caring about someone. Lucinda is such a delight, and I enjoy sharing her daily routine due to your cast. But I like to think that you would have let me do it anyway."

"Of course, Lucy. I am glad you have become a part of my baby's life. Someone to share in my motherhood experience. You have made us both so welcome. I couldn't have done it as well alone. I was dreading being in that house with Lionel and the baby. Although, I had never let on to anyone. I spent my days devoted to keeping the place impeccably clean to perfection. But secretly, I had a fear. With the baby needing attention, I wasn't sure that I could meet Lionel's high standards anymore." Diana shuddered at the thought of the cruel consequences she endured in the past.

"Lucinda would always have to be clean and dressed prettily to measure up. I was never sure that I could keep both the baby and the house the way Lionel expected of me any longer, and there would have been cruel reprisals."

"Diana, that is terrible. I understand now why you do some of the things you do. The way you keep everything tidy but not perfectly straight. I can appreciate that now. We should have had this talk a lot sooner." Lucy went to the cupboards and haphazardly arranged all the cans while Diana laughed in relief at Lucy's response to her story.

Diana felt like she had found a true friend and a sister. She was happy that Troy had thought of his sister for her refuge in her need for a home.

She noticed that Lucy responded to her presence in the house, singing a lot. Lucy's laughter rained so spontaneously. Yes, this was a good change of direction in her young life.

Diana didn't let her mind include Tory. She wasn't ready to dwell on their so-called relationship. But a brother was definitely out of the equation for Diana, she secretly thought.

Lucy had made a cup of tea to end their evening. Lucinda was tucked in her crib.

Lucy and Diana were sharing girl talk about their teens and the boyfriends that might've been. Lucy was keeping the conversation light and nonsensical. She was sure Diana had never had the opportunity to share these types of tidbits with anyone.

Diana even came up with the story of a teenaged boy that had caught her eye. But every time he was near, she either dropped her books or tripped over nothing in particular. So, she felt sure he only thought of her as a klutz. They both laughed merrily over her comic description of herself during her shy teen years.

"Troy was very personable and easygoing. He never lacked male or female friends. Troy just seemed never to have found the right girl to trigger his heart. His male friends looked at me as a kid that never got lost. I wanted to be noticed, so I made myself very evident whenever they came over to our place. Troy accepted her presence, but his buddies didn't."

Lucy even included some of the ways that several girls tried to get Troy's attention. "There was this one girl. She kept trying to bribe me to invite her over when Troy was home. I made sure Troy would be out. Then I would invite her over after I accepted her bribe. We would sit and talk. She preened to strike the perfect pose to get Troy's attention, but he never came home. After three times, she finally got the message. I never returned her bribes." Lucy chuckled, remembering that one.

The morning came too soon after their late-night chat exchange and Lucinda having a restless night. Lucy and Diana both arrived in the kitchen, blurry-eyed groping for the coffee they could smell.

"Well, well, aren't you both looking bright-eyed and bushy-tailed? Were you two binging after we left last night?" Troy was sitting in the chair with Lucinda comfortably lying in his arms, sipping his coffee.

Diana snapped to attention. "Lucinda wasn't crying, was she?"

"No, she was stirring when I arrived. So, I changed her diaper and brought her down here. We were exchanging baby talk. She told me you two had a very late-night."

"Right, Troy. Diana and I had a wonderful evening trading girl talk. You were one of our most interesting subjects. Isn't that right, Diana?" Lucy was waking up after a few sips of coffee. Her humor was the usual bantering.

"Well, Troy did prove to be one interesting subject we covered." Diana smilingly joined in.

"Was she good to me, Diana? How else could she have been? I was the perfect brother."

"Right, Troy. The perfect brother?" But Lucy's laugh said otherwise.

Troy ended the talk in self-defense by asking, "what's for breakfast? I know what Lucinda wants, but it's my stomach that is my concern. Here mama." He held out Lucinda as she made noises of wanting special attention that Troy was incapable of producing.

Diana accepted Lucinda with a blush. She couldn't expose herself like she usually did while Lucy made breakfast. So, she exited the room.

Lucy called out, "Diana come back here. Troy, you behave yourself. Quit embarrassing Diana. You'll get an omelet for breakfast."

Diana arrived back in the kitchen with a light blanket covering the nursing Lucinda. Her cheeks were glowing with the blush that was deeper now under Troy's watchful eyes.

"I can't believe you are still embarrassed when I am around so often like family," Troy said gently to her.

Diana's glow of red deepened. She never thought of Troy as family, at least not as a brother.

Lucy came to her aid. To defuse the situation, she asked, "how come you're here so early? Didn't you have rounds at the hospital this morning?"

"Yes, but I decided to do them later while Diana was getting her cast removed." Troy wished Lucy hadn't interrupted. He would like to have known her response to his comment on family. Was it a brother or otherwise? Now he would never know.

Lucy placed a fluffy omelet in front of Troy, giving him an endearing look. It was nice to have a man to cook for, even if it was her brother.

Diana couldn't eat until she changed her arm around Lucinda. So, Troy picked up her fork. He lifted some omelet to her mouth. She opened her mouth obediently while they looked deeply into each other's eyes. They broke their gaze when Lucinda let her know she was ready for the change. Lucy usually helped her. Diana's face was flustered again as Troy reached forward, whipping Lucinda around to her other arm as though it was all perfectly natural. He then draped the baby blanket over her once again. Diana fumbled to cover one breast before exposing the other to Lucinda's questing mouth.

When Lucinda settled greedily suckling, Diana gave her attention back to her omelet. But Troy had picked up the fork and held some fluffy cheese omelet out to her lips. She opened her mouth, but she didn't meet his eyes this time.

She murmured when she could, "I can do it now, Troy."

Diana avoided his face but removed her fork from his hand. Their fingers touched. A spark of electricity ran through them, but neither acknowledged the instant zing.

Lucy filled the gap. "Diana, I bet you are going to be so happy to get rid of that old cast. To be able to use your arm normally." She had noticed the endearing blushes between Diana and her brother. It was the first time she had observed any reaction to each other of intimacy. Was something developing between these two?

"It is hard to believe it is eight weeks already. Oh, yes. It will make my life so much simpler. I'll be able to do so much more without requiring assistance. I'll be able to take over the housework that I was supposed to do to earn my keep."

"I don't even think about that," Lucy replied. She had never told Diana that Troy had been helping pay for her keep. He had never wanted Diana to know. Lucy had told him it wasn't necessary. But he had insisted on doing his part, having asked her to take Diana and Lucinda into her home.

"I certainly will feel better. I feel we are imposing on you," admitted Diana.

"Look, just having someone here with me has made all the difference to me. Isn't that right, Troy?"

"Yeah. Lucy was pining her life away. The difference you and Lucinda have made in her life is worth your keep for years to come. I am not spoofing. I was anxious about Lucy with no end in sight until you came into her life. You and Lucinda have been a godsend."

Their words gratified Diana. But she felt Lucy had saved her. Now, they were telling her she and her baby had saved Lucy. Apparently, they had saved each other.

Lucy hugged Diana. Troy joined in, hugging them both. Then everyone laughed.

"I hate to break this up. But we need to leave Diana."

Diana passed the fed and burped baby over to Lucy. Diana went to prepare for the trip to the hospital.

Troy delivered Diana to the lab for the removal of her cast. Then he whizzed away saying, he would be back in approximately an hour. Diana ventured inside, letting the nurse know her name. She was early. The nurse said, "you'll have to wait until the man ahead of you finishes."

Diana automatically looked over towards the wheelchair. The doctor had cut off the man's leg cast. In a volunteer's candy stripe uniform, a young girl took the chair handles to direct the chair out of the room. Diana's eyes beheld the patient, and to her horror, it was Lionel.

Lionel was looking down at his unwrapped leg, so he didn't notice her. She was relieved. Except that Diana's name was announced as the next outpatient to have the cast removed.

Lionel's head whipped around. "YOU! How dare you come near me." Then looking around, he announced to the room at large. "This vile woman abandoned me because I had my leg removed. She was my wife. I haven't seen nor heard from her since our car accident, which she caused." Then looking at Diana directly, he continued, "how do you sleep nights knowing you have abandoned your loving husband because he has no leg? God should strike you dead."

Diana looked horror-struck as though shot. There were several nurses, a couple of doctors, and one other patient present in the room. They were all staring at her.

"God will get you, Diana. God will get you." Lionel was yelling. The candy striper froze on the spot. One of the doctors sizing up a wicked situation leaped forward, pushing the stunned girl aside, and rolled the wheelchair from the room. The candy striper, calmed by the doctor's action, followed them. Immediately, everyone was looking elsewhere, trying to avoid looking at Diana. She was crying. She wanted to run and never stop.

A nurse nudged her towards the chair with a unique armrest for the cast. Diana sunk lower in humiliation. Her face was red under her escaping tears, wanting to yell the truth. 'Lionel, that man has abandoned our baby daughter and kidnapped me. The truth of the car accident was Lionel was evading the police in a car chase.' But everyone was avoiding looking at her.

So, she was made guilty by Lionel's words accepted as the truth. Unable to defend herself, Diana was numb. The doctor and nurse were business-like as they attended her cast removal. Neither meeting her eyes or acknowledging her tears. After the release of her arm, the doctor suggested physiotherapy. Then he walked away from her. The nurse called the next patient.

Diana arose from the chair, cradling her newly exposed arm. She slunk from the room. Before the door closed behind her, Diana heard the buzz of voiced comments adding onto Lionel's statement, which cut off as the door swung closed. She felt shattered. Lionel and his vile mouth, destroying a beautiful happy day.

Diana wanted to run away, but she knew Troy was to pick her up near the nurse's station down the hall. There were some seats nearby where she sat down.

One of the nurses appeared that had been in the room at the time of Lionel's pronouncement. She stopped at the nurse's station. There was whispering, then glances in Diana's direction.

How could she live through this embarrassment? How much longer would Troy be? The carrier of tales nurse disappeared. Diana went over to the other nurse. She had no choice. "Excuse me? Do you know Dr. Sawyer?"

"Yes." The expression on the nurse's face was not friendly.

"Would you please tell Dr. Sawyer that Diana will be out in the parking lot?"

She quickly turned away as the nurse affirmed. "The information will be passed on to him."

Her footsteps were fleeting as she nearly ran from the hospital. She stood leaning against Troy's car crying. Her sobbing became uncontrollable. How could Lionel do this to her? The tale would be all over the hospital in no time the way the nurses were gossiping. "Please, Troy, come and take me home."

When Troy arrived running, he grabbed her shoulders, swinging her around. "Oh, Diana, I am so sorry." He pulled her into his chest, hugging her.

"You heard?" she accused.

"Yes, Diana. At first, I didn't realize the nurses' gossip was about you because I just heard them talking about some horrible woman abandoning her husband after his accident. It wasn't until I heard the name Diana Cardwell that I realized they were talking about you and Lionel."

Diana started crying again.

"Diana, I straightened them out quickly, explaining the true story. I also demanded the gossipers correct the story to all personnel involved in the spreading of the falsehood. Plus, I told the doctor who removed your cast the truth. He is a good friend of mine. He will correct the others on the actual events." He pulled Diana away from his chest. Her tears were drying at his explanation of his amendments to the gossip.

"Diana, that is why I took so long getting here. Look at me," he ordered.

Diana raised her eyes.

"I should have realized that Lionel would be getting his cast removed today also. After all, you both got them on the same day. It was just coincidental that your appointments coincided. I would never have let this happen if I had known." He kissed both her cheeks. His lips absorbed her tears under his grazing kisses. Then he drew her back into his arms as though he was protecting her from any further unpleasantness.

"Let's go home. Lucinda and Lucy are waiting."

Troy released her to open the car door. He gently eased her inside. Troy whipped around the car to slide in beside her. He engaged the ignition. The powerful vehicle glided from the parking lot.

Diana felt the nasty gossip within the hospital was still running rampant, even though Troy had tried to defuse it.

"Diana, this is not your fault. It should never have happened. I didn't think about the possibility of running into Lionel. We know the truth. Some of the nurses know the truth, such as Nurse Spiegel and nurses with you on 5West. They will correct the gossip too.

The knowledge that some did know the truth made the situation bearable. Such as Mr. Gerard knows the truth, and so do the police.

Troy had come to Lucy's one day with the news that the police were charging Lionel with attempted kidnapping and abandonment of his baby. The case was to be held after Lionel left the hospital. The police had come to get Diana and Troy's statements on the matter.

Diana knew she had to put this latest attack by Lionel behind her. She wanted her homecoming to be in the same vein as when she had left. She looked down at her arm. The freedom was delightful, flexing her left arm and fingers.

Troy noticed. He knew she had removed the shroud over her at last. He put his hand out to clasp Diana's soft, tender hand.

"How does it feel? Ready to take on the world?" Troy smiled.

Diana was looking at the hand linked with hers. Her heart was singing.

"It feels wonderful," pausing. "Really wonderful."

Troy wondered about the look on her face as she gazed at their clasped hands. Was that part of the reason for the double wonderful? He squeezed her hand gently. "How does that feel?"

Diana's face broke into a smile. She raised her eyes to look at Troy.

“My hand and arm feel great. I am pleased to have the use of my arm again,” she said warmly.

“We have to link you up with a therapist and start the proper exercises required to strengthen your arm and hand.”

“Will I be able to do them on my own, or will I have to go somewhere often?”

“Once the therapist gives you a set of exercises, they can be done at home. But they will want to see you occasionally to check your progress. Why?”

“I need to be home for Lucinda and to do the housework expected of me by Lucy to earn my keep.”

Troy removed his hand quickly when he made a fast lane change because a careless driver had pulled out into traffic in front of them without checking correctly.

Diana’s hand felt chilled without Troy’s encircling warm hand.

Chapter Eight

Lucy was waiting at the door with Lucinda.

Diana looked fearful. "Was she a problem? I thought she would sleep while I was gone." Lucinda looked peaceful in Lucy's arms.

"No, she has been sleeping. I heard her stirring. So, I took the opportunity to lift her into my arms. It feels so good to have a baby in my arms again." She was smiling broadly.

Troy inquired, "do you have any coffee on?"

"Yes, knowing the way you function on coffee. I made a fresh pot." Lucy led the way to the kitchen after they removed their jackets.

"Lucy, I do love your coffee. The way you blend the beans makes for a wonderful bouquet." Troy savored the coffee with each sip.

"Diana, how did the removal of the cast go?" inquired Lucy.

Troy leaped in. "Doesn't Lucinda need to be changed or fed, Diana?"

Lucinda was squirming now. Diana took her daughter into her arms, walking upstairs to the baby's room. Only too glad for the opportunity to avoid the incident at the hospital.

Lucinda's smiled at her while she changed her. The baby was blowing bubbles and kicking with her feet. Freedom from the hampering diaper, Diana was watching her kick. She noticed Lucinda's legs appeared to be straighter than when she was born. Her heart jumped with the knowledge that what Troy had said might possibly happen had. She would have to tell the others. Maybe Lucinda wouldn't need an operation after all. Her heart was lighter with this new probability.

Diana sat in the rocker while Lucinda nursed. She crooned a little song as she contentedly rocked.

Troy gave Lucy an account of Lionel's behavior at the hospital.

Lucy was stunned. "How could he do that to her? Poor Diana. I hope you put a stop to that gossip, straightening everyone out to the truth of the situation. I know what the gossip mills are like in places like that."

"Of course. I made the staff aware of Diana's true story. The nurses on 5West can rectify the gossip also. I was horrified to hear what had happened. Of course, Lionel would have his leg cast removed today. I just never dreamed it would be at the same time."

"How is she now?"

"I think she has come to grips with it after I explained that I have stopped the gossip. I am sure this only confirmed her decision to leave Lionel was the right one more than ever."

"That is terrible, Troy. She didn't deserve that at all. Now, I can understand how he could reject his baby. A man like that has no morals. Diana is better off away from him. With the removal of her cast, she has no reason to go near the hospital."

"That is what I have been thinking. Now, let's drop the subject before Diana gets back. She doesn't need any reminders."

"Troy, do you remember Mark's friend Eric that used to breeze into town every once in a while? He is a pilot with Jetway. He arrived into town last night."

"Yeah, I remember him. He used to visit an aunt or something. Then he would visit you and Mark. So, he got in touch with you?"

"Yes, while you were at the hospital. Eric wants to take me out for dinner. Why don't you and Diana come too?"

"Not this time. You have to start going out on your own sometime. Eric came for Mark and Connor's funeral, I remember."

"Yes, he did. I don't know whether I'm ready for male companionship yet."

"Of course, you are. It should be more natural for you because Eric is a friend. You and Mark have known him for years. Besides, I think you are ready to pick up your social life again. I was worried about you before Diana came. But now you are much better. It is time."

"Yes, Diana and Lucinda have made me less lonely. So, I don't dwell on Mark and Connor's passing quite so much. It was the many memories in the house that kept me in a continual state of depression. I gave away Mark's belongings, but I couldn't do anything about Connor's things until Lucinda needed the space. She is such a happy baby, just like Connor was, and she happily responds to me. You have no idea how much that did for me than anything else. Thank you for bringing them here."

"Now, you know why I brought them here. I was so worried about you. You were hanging onto your loss for far too long. Working at home the way you do, didn't get you away from the situation. That was why I kept trying to talk you into an office away from home."

"You don't have to worry anymore. My business is expanding. Women's groups have been contacting me to give talks on my form of protocol on women's issues and the legalities. I am even considering doing seminars. As well, I provide info over the Internet which reaches all over the world."

"Good, I always thought you would be great at something like that. When you came up with this idea for your business, I thought it wouldn't be successful. It was just a form of occupying yourself while Connor was keeping you home. But it has been a success for you, that's good."

"You are right. Maybe I did start it to keep my hand into something besides Mark and Connor. But I believe in what I am doing as well. Now, I am more serious since it has been getting such a positive response lately. This subject was what I wrote my thesis on at university. So, I know the subject backward and forwards. I have added to my knowledge through the Internet. I put it into layman's language, which has triggered my mailings to triple."

"That is good. Now, back to Eric. I think you should go out and enjoy yourself. You are long overdue. I will come over later to keep Diana company. So, you won't have to rush home."

"Okay, I'll try it. But don't be surprised if I bring Eric here after dinner when the conversation skills peter out."

"It's like rolling off a log. Once you let yourself relax, it comes easily. Now enjoy."

Troy looked towards the door as Diana appeared with Lucinda. "Hi, all fed?"

"Yes, she seems to be fussing. So, I thought I would bring her down for a while."

"Pass her to me. Then you can get a coffee." Troy held out his arms for Lucinda.

Diana slipped her daughter into his waiting arms. "Troy, her legs are straightening. I can see it."

Troy cleared a space on the table. He laid the blanketed baby down, uncovering her so she could kick freely. "Yes, her legs are definitely straighter. I'm thinking over time they will straighten completely. I did say she might correct the situation as her bones formed more solidly. She may have to wear braces for a while. But it won't mean an operation if she continues, which is good news. Your baby is going to be just fine." Tickling Lucinda's bare tummy as he lifted her shirt. Lucinda let out a baby giggle.

"Oh, Diana, this is good news," Lucy said.

"Yes, I am happy about it too." Diana broke out into a big grin.

Troy was watching Diana's face now that he had Lucinda encased in his arms. Diana is so pretty when she smiles. Her brown eyes were a blaze of light. He wished he could keep her smiling this way always.

Lucy had put a cup of coffee in front of Diana. She sat down to enjoy these friends and their easy companionship. They had made her feel like family. She avoided Troy's eyes that were almost devouring her, or so it seemed. Maybe he was just so happy about Lucinda. That was it, wasn't it?

Troy divulged, "do you know about Lucy's new beau? She has a date with Eric tonight."

Diana's gaze swung to Lucy to see how she was taking her brother's teasing. She knew Lucy had been avoiding any male social life. "That is wonderful. Who is Eric?"

"Eric is someone Mark and I have known for years. He used to breeze into town to visit his aunt. Then Eric would pop over to see us. He was Mark's friend. Sometimes, they went out to do the man thing while he was here as well."

"That's perfect. You're going out. You need that in your life." Diana was happy for Lucy.

"Yes, long overdue, Sis. Diana, I have to work late. But I'll drop in on my way home." Troy assured her.

"You don't have to do that. I will be all right on my own."

"I am coming, so be prepared. I know you can be on your own. But I want to make sure Lucy hasn't any excuse for coming home early from her date," giving Lucy a brotherly poke and a wide grin.

"I know how to conduct myself in public. I haven't been on the shelf that long that I will run home in a panic," Lucy laughed.

Troy's teasing was to help her get over her fright of the idea of going out with Eric. It would be the first time since Mark's funeral.

"Well, I have to work if you girls don't. This wee darling has gone off to sleep."

Diana quickly jumped up to take Lucinda from Troy.

"It's the man's touch she needed today," Troy commented with a special smile for Diana. That had nothing to do with the baby's sleeping.

Lucy observed the smile. Brother, you are smitten with this woman. Was that a good thing or not? He had been the proverbial bachelor for too long. It was hard to think of him as married. However, marriage was out of the question until Diana divorced Lionel. After today's experience with Lionel, Diana may make it sooner than later.

**

The days flew by. Diana had settled down to a routine with Lucinda and the house duties. But she never kept the perfection that Lionel required in his meticulous quest for exactness. Thankfully, Lucy didn't need it.

They had settled down to a routine. Troy, appearing quite often for meals and outings with Lucy, Diana, and Lucinda. Sometimes, it included Eric because Lucy and he had regularly seen each other since their first date together. Eric wasn't pressing Lucy into any commitment. However, you could see his commitment to their relationship by his frequent visits, hoping for a future.

Lucinda was growing. She was sharing smiles, reaching for objects, and recognizing them. Lucinda showed a preference for Troy when he was around. Pleasing Diana, as Troy was probably the closest to a father that Lucinda would ever have.

Life was breezing along. Lots of laughter permeated the house. Diana and Lucinda were flourishing in their happy home. Every time Diana mentioned getting a job, Lucy would raise her spending money, funneled through Lucy by Troy. He wanted Diana to have the experience of sharing Lucinda's baby years without working away from home.

Lucy had delegated all the housework to Diana so that she would feel needed.

Diana didn't want to leave this happy home. She knew when and if she got a job, she would have to make a life for herself and Lucinda elsewhere. So, she would let the problem slide each time Lucy increased her wage.

Lucy was taking on more seminars. She enjoyed speaking at the sessions away from home. Eric made a point of showing up for at least one night, then whiz her out to dinner. He commented that he didn't want her to get lonely when she was away from home. After a couple of months, he started sleeping over. Lucy wasn't letting on to Diana and Troy. But the way she came home beaming told its own story.

Troy would drop in while Lucy was away. Supposedly to check on Diana to see if she needed anything. Lucinda was sitting up and teething by this time. Troy would pacify the baby by rubbing her gums and holding her cold teething ring, giving Diana a break from Lucinda's discomfort.

Life was almost perfect.

Then the calls began. Lionel had found out her number from Diana's parents, being the staid people they were.

Diana only made duty calls to her parents because Lucinda was their only grandchild. But their lectures were always the same. They believed Diana should be with her husband because Lucinda needed her father, ignoring Lionel's refusal of Lucinda. They didn't think Lucy and Troy made up for the baby's father in Lucinda's life.

At first, the calls from Lionel were begging for forgiveness, with crying included. Then the demands became more aggressive, demanding Diana come home. His one call revealed his progress with his legs and their improvement, making him more independent. He was back working. He finished that they could have a normal life again.

Diana was changing with each call. She was getting quieter and quieter. She wasn't letting on to Lucy and Troy the number of calls she was receiving.

Lionel recognized when she wasn't alone by the tone of her voice. Then he kept the call brief until he could find her alone. Then the threats of dire consequences started if she didn't come home.

Troy and Lucy knew something was going on because Diana's eyes were getting listless. Gone was the sparkle in her and that carefree, happy manner.

At first, Lucy thought it was because she was going away too much with her seminars. Then, she shared with Troy that she thought Diana wanted and needed a job out in the workforce. A life for herself and Lucinda. So, they both started making comments along those lines. Suggestions for jobs she might be able to do.

Diana took it to mean Lucy wanted her gone from the house. Which only added to her receding spirit along with each horrible phone call.

She was having trouble finding an appetite. It was a good thing Diana was not nursing the baby anymore, or Lucinda would be starving.

The laughter was going out of her life. Unfortunately, Lucy was away more. Troy seemed not to drop in as frequently by design or otherwise. Diana didn't know.

Then one day, after one of Lionel's threatening calls, he showed up at the house. Diana was glad Lucy was away. She invited him in, hoping to talk about changing the situation. She noticed his funny gait caused by his prosthetic leg and the limp in the other. But he was able to maneuver around quite quickly. He wasn't interested in the baby. He made her put Lucinda to bed. So, they could talk freely.

Lucinda went to bed without a fuss. Meanwhile, Diana tried to steel her nerves about having Lionel in the house. She wasn't successful. Diana returned to the kitchen with dread. At first, she thought he had left because the kitchen seemed empty. Then she felt her neck grabbed from behind.

Chapter Nine

"Diana, you will do as I say. You will come home with me," squeezing her neck for emphasis. Diana grabbed at his hands, trying to free herself. She was having trouble breathing. Then he pushed her, and she fell to the floor. He kicked her in the ribs. Then bent over to whack her in the same area. She realized he kept his brutality so that no marks would be evident to people when they were around.

"Are you ready to do what I say?"

"No, Lionel," she said in a raspy voice.

Again, he kicked her, except this time he lost his balance and fell. He was pathetic, trying to regain his feet. The more he tried, the more he yelled and threatened her. This raging man was a new Lionel to her. He was not controlled like he used to be. The humiliation was making him angry.

Diana scurried out of his reach, holding onto her ribs. She was in control now. "Lionel, you had better leave, or I call 911." She had the receiver in her hand, ready to dial.

At last, Lionel had managed to regain his feet with the help of a chair and the table.

"This isn't the last. I will be back, and you will come home, Diana." He lurched out of the front door with a more pronounced limping gait. He must have hurt his leg when he fell. She didn't let go of the phone until she heard his car spin its wheels as he peeled into traffic.

Then she went to the bathroom to undress to assess the damage. Lucy would be home soon. Diana didn't think Lionel broke her ribs, feeling them. She had a cold shower trying to get rid of the bruising. Then a hot one to ease the pain. She put on a tight turtleneck sweater, hoping that would help strap her ribs. Because of her lack of appetite, she had lost weight. Her body looked pathetically thin in the clinging sweater. Even her full breasts from Lucinda's birth had receded.

Maybe she should wear something looser. She looked at the bedside clock. There wasn't time. She had to get down to the kitchen to hide the evidence of Lionel's visit. In his pulling himself up action, Lionel had knocked over some dishes and coffee on the table.

She raced to the kitchen. She cleaned the mess on the table and straightened the chairs carefully, moving her body as little as possible to alleviate the pain in her ribs.

She started dinner, deciding that a casserole was the easiest, throwing together ingredients and shoving them into the oven. She hoped Troy didn't intend to come tonight for dinner. This was the first time Diana had not wanted to see him. She always enjoyed his company and noticeably missed Troy.

Lucinda was crying. So, she went to attend to her, bringing her to the kitchen. It hurt to carry Lucinda from the bedroom. She was thankful Lucinda could sit in her highchair and entertain herself while the dinner cooked.

Lucy breezed in from her seminar. "Hi, Diana. Hi, my lovely." Lucy bent over to kiss Lucinda with her face up for Lucy's kissing ritual with her after work.

The two women idly chatted.

"Lucy, how was your day?" Diana was trying to move as little as possible because of the pain in her ribs. Hoping Lucy wouldn't notice the lack of movement. Lucy mostly played with Lucinda, thankfully.

"Fine. How much time do I have? I would like to change into something more relaxing."

"As long as you want. Dinner is in the oven keeping warm," Diana said sweetly but raspy, her throat hurt from Lionel's squeezing. She just hoped Lucy was not listening too intently.

Hearing Diana's reply, Lucy headed for the bedroom.

Unbeknownst to Diana, Lucy had come back into the room. Diana was holding her side and making a painful face as she set the table. When Diana became aware that Lucy was there, her face changed. She patted her sweater like it was clinging too tightly. Lucy didn't say anything. But she secretly watched her after that.

"How was your day, Diana?"

"Same as usual, housework and Lucinda." replying as sweetly as possible.

"That boring? Diana, you should get out more. The weather is much warmer. Lucinda would like to go to the playground or mall. Don't you have any girlfriend you can visit?"

"No, Lionel, never encouraged me to have friends, and neither did my parents."

"Well, you might meet someone at the playground, three blocks over. The one I showed you recently. You know you don't have to spend your whole day doing housework."

"I have been to the playground. I did meet a couple of ladies one day. But you pay me to do the housework."

"Diana, I thought you had been here long enough to feel like family, not a paid servant. You are getting quite pale-looking as of late. If you don't have any friends, who are making the phone calls? You said they were from friends."

"Not friends, but acquaintances of my parents checking to see if I'm okay. Because my parents think I don't call them enough." Diana hoped Lucy didn't wonder why her parents weren't phoning themselves. She didn't want to let on that it was Lionel.

"I thought Troy would have called in tonight. He knew I would be home. He hasn't been coming as much lately." Lucy was watching Diana's reaction to that. She had felt something was developing between the two of them.

"Yes, I noticed. Maybe, Troy has a new lady friend. After all, he is a bachelor." Diana tried for nonchalance. She had been wondering the same thing but not mentioning it because of Lionel.

"Perhaps, but I don't think so. Troy would have told me, I am sure."

Diana moved too quickly. She let out a gasp.

"Is something wrong, Diana?"

"Mm . . . just a stitch in my side." Diana rose gingerly to get the dessert and tea. Lucy was watching her. There was definitely something wrong with the way Diana was moving. She wished Troy would come, so she could ask him what he thought.

After dinner, they watched television. Lucinda was playing on the floor. When it was time to take Lucinda to bed, Diana bent over to pick her up. She had to grit her teeth at the excruciating pain. But she did manage without a moan. Any other night, Lucy offered to put Lucinda to bed. But not tonight. Diana would never purposely ask her.

Instead of her usual bath, Diana gave her just a wash. Then changed her into her bunny pajamas, intending to put her in her crib. Quite often, when it was bedtime, Lucy would come in to say goodnight. Lucy didn't put in an appearance. So, Lucinda put up a fuss wanting Lucy, wiggling her arms and legs.

"Please, Lucinda, don't fight me. It hurts too much."

"What hurts too much?" Troy's voice shocked Diana. She whipped around, and the pain almost made her double over.

"Oh . . . Lucinda was just giving me a hard time about going to bed. That is all."

Troy came over to take Lucinda, tickling her and lifting her over his head. She was laughing. Then he dropped her face down to his. Lucinda gave him a smacking kiss.

"Now, little lady, it is time for bed. Kiss your mommy. Then it's into bed." Troy leaned Lucinda out towards Diana, Lucinda kissed her. Then Troy put her in the crib and covered her. "Sleep tight, little one," caressing her face.

He followed Diana from the room, noting the slimness of her due to her weight loss. Lucy had told him that Diana seemed to be walking gingerly. How could he find out the problem?

They proceeded down the stairs. Troy reached out as if to grab the railing but grazed her body. Diana sort of flinched, which caused her to let out a groan. She quickly recovered.

"Diana, would you make me a coffee? Your coffee is so good. I look forward to it when I come here."

Diana walked towards the kitchen with Troy trailing behind.

"Lucy must still be watching TV." Troy stood in the doorway, watching Diana's movements. "How have you been, Diana?"

"Fine, why do you ask?" She watched his expression to see if he had guessed her problem after what had happened on the stairs.

"No reason. I just haven't been here for a while. That is all." He came up behind her as she removed a mug from the cupboard. He leaned close, touching his lips to the side of her neck. Diana jumped and let out a gasp of pain.

"Diana, is there something wrong?"

"No, I just didn't expect that endearment. Why did you kiss me?"

"Because I haven't seen you for a while. I felt in a friendly mood. Troy's arm encircled Diana before she could move, enclosing around her midriff, pulling her against him. This time it was a loud gasp as pain shot through her. Then he knew there was a problem.

"Diana, how did you hurt yourself?"

"Hurt myself? What are you talking about?" She wanted to remove his arm but was not able to without hurting herself. But she should have as he tightened his arm that was encircling her. She gave out a cry which she could not control.

Troy whipped up her sweater before she could move away, showing the bruises where Lionel had kicked her. Troy ran his hands over her ribs. She could not conceal the pain.

"Who did this?"

"I fell against the wall."

He had pulled her around so he could see both sides and the front. "Diana, not when the bruising is on both sides. I won't buy that. Diana, was Lionel here? He kicked you in the ribs, didn't he? Don't bother to deny it."

Diana let her tears fall, not replying.

Troy was feeling her ribs, trying to determine if any were broken. "You should have them X-rayed."

"They aren't that bad." She was embarrassed at being touched so intimately, even if he was a doctor. Her stomach was doing flip-flops going between intimacy and humiliation at his touch.

"Diana, why did you let Lionel enter? Is he the one that has been phoning you? You said the calls were coming from a friend of your parents."

"I didn't want to let on Lionel was calling. My parents gave him my phone number. I didn't think he knew where I lived. I kept telling him that I wasn't coming home."

Troy pulled her gently into his arms, letting her cry. The tears were cascading down her cheeks. He kissed her forehead, then each eye trying to stem the flow.

"Why didn't you tell us? I would've talked with him. Diana, you are not to let Lionel in here ever again."

"I didn't want him carrying on where Lucy's neighbors could see him."

"Did he do anything to Lucinda?"

"No. Lionel didn't even want to see her. He wanted me to go with him, knocking me down. Then kicked me twice when I refused him. He hurt his leg when he fell. That let me have the upper hand, and I grabbed the telephone, intending to call 911. He quickly left then. Otherwise, I don't know what he would have done."

"We should get the police in to report this."

"No, Troy. It is too embarrassing."

"Diana, they have to know for the record. He has already kidnapped you once." Troy went to the phone to call the police. In response, they were sending someone right away.

Lucy put in an appearance, hearing the explanation to the police Troy was giving over the phone.

"Oh, Diana, why didn't you tell me Lionel has been bothering you?"

"I thought he just had my phone number. I didn't know he had my address. My parents must have told him. They think I am wrong and that my place is with my husband regardless."

"Yes, but what do they think about the fact that Lucinda doesn't appear to be welcome in his home?" Troy inquired with concern.

"They think my first concern should be my husband and not my baby. But then they never wanted me either. After I was born, they endured me as a child to be seen and not heard."

"That is terrible," said Troy. "Lucy, can you postpone your trips away from home for a while?"

"Of course. Now that I know what is going on, I will stay put. I have enough work to keep me busy here for quite a while. No way will Lionel get in here again."

Diana came out of her humiliation. "No, Lucy, you can't give up your seminars for me. I won't have that."

"Fine, then I move in while Lucy is away," Troy said insistently. "Have you spent any time at the playground where you could meet other mothers yet?"

"Yes," said Diana in self-defense. "I have met two mothers that take their children on Tuesdays and Thursdays for sure and sometimes Friday."

"Good, then if and when I need to work those particular days, I will drop you off at the park. You stay with them until I get back. Do they stay long?"

"Not sometimes, but I could walk with them to their place. I could let you know so you can pick me up there." Not wanting any of this, which would inconvenience them because of her problem.

The doorbell rang. Officer Jackson and Officer Thompson came in. "We thought we recognized the name." Troy led them into the kitchen, where Diana and Lucy were sitting.

"Hello, Mrs. Cardwell. I hear you have a problem." Officer Jackson stated.

"Yes, my husband came to visit me," she answered, embarrassed to the teeth.

"I believe it was more than a visit from what I hear from Dr. Sawyer."

"Well, Lionel was upset with me for not going with him."

Officer Jackson took out his notebook. "Let's start from the beginning, shall we?"

"Do you want coffee?" Lucy asked the officers.

"No, ma'am, not while we are on duty," replied Officer Thompson.

"Now, Mrs. Cardwell, I understand your husband has been phoning you for a while now?" inquired Officer Jackson.

"Yes, I guarded my speech when either Lucy or Troy was here. Then Lionel keeps the calls brief, knowing someone is nearby. But if they weren't here, he was quite open in what he had to say."

"How did he get your phone number?"

"From my parents. They believe I have a commitment to Lionel because of my marriage vows. So, I am sure they gave my phone number and address to him."

"What about the baby? If I remember correctly, her name was Lucinda." Officer Jackson questioned.

"Yes, Lucinda."

"How is the little darling faring?"

"Oh, she is doing well. Her legs have been straightening as her bones get stronger. Instead of an operation, Troy thinks it may mean only braces for a while. We are hopeful," proclaimed Diana.

"That is wonderful to hear. I remember Lucinda was a cute wee girl."

"Yes, Officer, and she is getting cuter every day," Lucy chimed in.

"We would like to have seen her. I guess she is in bed," said Officer Thompson inquiringly.

"Yes, she is sleeping."

"Now, Mrs. Cardwell, back to the questioning. How did Mr. Cardwell react to Lucinda?"

"He wanted no part of her. He insisted I put her to bed before he talked to me."

"It sounds like he did more than talk from the explanation Dr. Sawyer gave me."

"Well, yes. I invited Lionel in only because I didn't want him making a spectacle in front of Lucy's neighbors. After putting Lucinda down for a nap, he started pushing me around because I said I had no intention of going with him. I fell on the floor, and Lionel kicked me in the ribs. He was a meticulous man, so he didn't like to put any abrasions on me that others could see." She looked fearfully at Troy for his reaction to this statement.

Troy's face was a picture of amazement. "You mean he has done this before? Diana, how could you have stayed with him?" Troy was angry now at Lionel's brutality to her.

"He didn't do it if I kept the house and myself in a state of perfection. So, I learned not to provoke his anger." Her eyes were pleading for Troy to understand.

"Mrs. Cardwell, after he kicked you, what happened then?" He was as angry as Dr. Sawyer, but he had to hide his feelings. He always hated domestic quarrels when macho men use their wives as punching bags or in this case, kicking.

"When I again didn't comply with his wishes, he punched me in the ribs where he had kicked me before. When I refused to leave with him still, he kicked me again, but this time he fell. Lionel has an artificial limb on his left leg and a limp in his right. He kicked me with his right leg. Lionel must have gotten off balance or something because he fell. Then he had to get up with the assistance of a chair and the table. It was unusual to see because he hated any weaknesses or imperfections. This caught my attention to his disability. Once he got up, he left without a word. Only yelling from the door that he would be back."

"Did you tell him about Lucinda's legs straightening?"

"No, he didn't want to hear about her in any way."

"You mean he still wanted you to leave without Lucinda?" Officer Jackson couldn't believe Lionel could still feel that way about Lucinda. Especially after the amputation of his left leg and the limp in his right.

"Yes, to him, Lucinda was not perfect. So, he didn't want her. That decision was made when Dr. Sawyer made his pronouncement at Lucinda's birth."

"Did your parents know this when they gave him your telephone number?"

"Yes, they thought my wedding vows, to love, honor and obey my husband were more important than my baby. You see, they never wanted me. It was an unexpected birth that did not enhance their marriage. They were devoted to each other and excluded me. They only loved each other."

"Even when you were growing up?" Officer Jackson was having trouble keeping his voice neutral hearing this young woman's story.

"Yes, I was seen but not heard. I was encouraged to spend most of my time in my bedroom. Even now, although I am an adult, I am hardly acknowledged. I told my parents about Lucinda's birth. I have only seen them a couple of times since she was born. They are not interested in their grandchild."

Troy felt terrible for Diana. She must be dying of embarrassment confessing her life with Lionel and her parents.

Lucy and Troy were exchanging sad looks in sympathy for Diana's upbringing. Troy now understood her earlier behavior when he first arrived.

"Mrs. Cardwell, what were your husband's phone calls like?"

"As I said, if he knew from my voice that Lucy or Troy were around, he was very brief."

"Yes, you said that, but what about the other calls?"

"In the beginning, he was pleasant and pleading. Then changed to demanding. Then threatening and demanding."

"Dr. Sawyer indicated that he knew nothing about the calls."

Diana looked at Troy pleadingly. "I didn't want him or Lucy to know. I hoped Lionel would give up without any unpleasantness because I didn't think he knew my address. But I should have known my parents would give him my address too. I was in denial, hoping Lionel would believe me and give up. But he didn't," she ended sadly.

She knew she had damaged her relationship with Troy and Lucy by not telling them about Lionel. These two, who had taken her and Lucinda so lovingly into their home and hearts.

Both officers could see the distress Mrs. Cardwell's story was having on the brother and sister. They cared for this young lady. Officer Jackson wanted to say, don't hold the hiding of Lionel's calls against her, being raised in an unloving family atmosphere where nobody listens or wants to listen to anything she has to say.

"Mrs. Cardwell, the police cannot do anything to stop your husband. Other than suggest that you might want to get a restraining order against him. Then we can stop him if he comes near you. You call 911 as soon as he arrives. We will respond quickly." He added to himself. *I hope it will be quick enough.* He hated these domestic cases. They so often ended in tragedy for the woman before they stopped the husband.

Troy leaped in. "Now that we know about Lionel's calls and his coming here. We will be here for her. We just didn't know."

Removing the hurt from his voice because Diana didn't need that on top of everything else.

The two officers stood, indicating there was no more that they could say or do. "Mrs. Cardwell, it was right to call us. Did you get your ribs X-rayed?"

"No, she wouldn't go. I felt them, but I think they are just badly bruised," said Troy with a tone in his voice that he just might take her to the hospital for his peace of mind.

"Well, we will make a report and put it in your file." The two officers were ready to leave. "Mr. Cardwell is building quite a case against himself. I don't believe his court case has reached the docket yet. At least, we haven't been informed as of yet."

Troy accompanied them to the door. Troy assured them that Lionel would never get near Diana again if he could help it. Either Lucy or himself would be here for her from now on.

"Be careful you don't offend him to the extent of squaring off. I don't want you involved in a court case. Mr. Cardwell is the type of man that will sue you to the hilt, and that will hamper our case against him." Officer Jackson said in an attempt to defuse this man's justified ire.

Lucy tried to assure Diana that she would be here for her. She was never to hold back information about Lionel again.

Lucy had Diana in her arms, hugging her as Troy reentered the room. Lucy was saying, "I knew something was wrong the way you were losing weight. You also seemed to be unhappy and not yourself. But when I asked, you never opened up to me."

"I didn't want to include you in Lionel's rage. I thought I could handle the phone calls myself. Why didn't I realize that he would eventually show up here?"

"Because you are a trusting person. Don't feel bad. But you must promise never to hold back anything again. You are part of our family now. A family looks out for family, isn't that right, Troy?"

"Yes, now I am taking you to the hospital to X-ray your ribs. I will feel much better if I have that attended to."

"But, Troy, I am fine." Diana grimaced as she jerked around.

"I am the doctor here. Please get ready as we are going. The police require the information." Troy ended trying to appease her.

They arrived back with Diana's ribs bound. They were still painful but felt better when she breathed to be tightly bound.

"Did he fracture your ribs?" Lucy greeted them.

"Yes, but only cracked two. Diana has strapped ribs until she heals. She has to be careful, lifting Lucinda for a while." Troy's hand touched Diana's back as they entered the living room. He could feel the strapping that encased her ribs, bringing to light his ire against Lionel once again.

"No problem. I can reduce my workload for a week. I have been working extra hard lately." Lucy eased Diana's mind with her quick answer.

"Now, she needs a cup of tea and some pain pills. Then she will be all set for bed."

"Yes, Dr. Troy," Diana tried to joke. She was trying to cover her shyness at being fussed over. Something she had never experienced except by these two loving people.

Diana thought that with the removal of the arm cast, their attitude would change. But here she was again being showered with kindness.

Troy made the tea and served Diana and Lucy, ensuring that Diana took her pills first. They talked about a strategy for handling Lionel's future calls knowing that there would be more. Lucy was to answer most of the telephone calls, even during working hours.

Lucy and Diana had a whistle to blow piercingly into the phone until Lionel understood that Lucy was not leaving Diana alone. Plus, letting him know that they would take no more nonsense from him.

Chapter Ten

Today, Diana rose feeling better. She was putting on some weight. Lionel hadn't called for a week. Her ribs felt better, so she had removed the strapping before her shower.

It had taken Lionel a week of calls before he got the message that Diana wasn't talking to him anymore. The first two times he experienced the whistle piercing his eardrums from Lucy and Diana made him super annoyed. He had kept phoning, but Lucy felt sure he held the receiver away from his ear each time.

Lucinda thought the whistle was a great game, clapping her hands and giggling. Troy had taught her to play pattycake. So, she clapped her hands when she saw him as well.

Troy was coming around when Lucy had to go out on business or socially with Eric. Lucinda and Troy formed a bond to the degree that Lucinda crawled to him as soon as he showed up. He had her standing and was trying to teach her to walk.

Diana felt sure he was trying to make her the youngest baby in history to walk. His excuse was, he wanted to see how her legs were reacting to the weight. Troy made her move her legs on her own but never let Lucinda go.

During these months of her life, Lucinda's legs had straightened remarkably. Troy now felt she might not need braces if this kept up. The next month or two should tell the tale. At Troy's insistence, Lucinda wore good shoes for walking. Lucinda wanted to walk all the time when Troy was there. But he never overdid the exercise.

"You little minx, you just want to walk to get my undivided attention." He picked her up, raising her over his head. As her little legs churned in excitement, they would both laugh.

Diana watched them, a little envious that her daughter had so much of Troy's attention. Why would she think that? Then Diana had to be honest. She was hopelessly in love with Troy, although he always acted more like a brother to her.

Diana never expected to be jealous. Besides, how could she share love with Troy? She was still married to Lionel. She had never thought about divorce until now. She wished she was free of him. Would Lionel object too strongly if she asked for her freedom? He had been out of her life for a week now. Did she want to stir up his anger again? No, she had better forget the divorce and her feelings for Troy. Besides, she had a feeling that there was already someone in his life. He had indicated that to Lucy one day.

Troy enjoyed her daughter. At least, Lucinda had a male in her life to respond to for a while.

Lucy's relationship with Eric was becoming quite involved. She seemed ten years younger after she had returned home from the latest seminar. Diana didn't feel Lucy could credit all that to the trip. Knowing Lucy's seminar schedule, Eric showed up for dinner and a night's stay each time. Diana felt bad that Lucy had curtailed her seminars since Lionel's unwelcome visit.

If only she could be sure Lionel was out of her life, she would be happy.

When she joined Lucy for coffee, Lucy kept slipping Eric's name into the conversation, which confirmed Diana's thoughts. Lucy was relating her last seminar's success.

Diana's thoughts were on her healing ribs which made her daily routine easier again. She and Lucinda were spending time walking to the park. She visited with the two women she knew there. Betty had a son Cowan, who was a little older than Lucinda's eight months. The other lady, Audrey, had a daughter, Nancy, two and a son, Nathan, three.

Diana was thankful that Audrey and Betty were at the park when she arrived today. They usually were there. Diana never let on about Lionel. She wasn't the type of person to share her private life. She always let Betty and Audrey provide most of the conversation.

Betty was a talker and seemed to possess the ability to control the chatting when they were all together. Diana just accepted that, as did Audrey. Diana contributed to the discussion when she could. So, that they wouldn't think she was standoffish.

Diana realized her mind had slipped away from Lucy's conversation. Lucy seemed to be waiting for an answer to a question that was hanging in the air. But Diana had no idea what it was.

"I'm sorry, Lucy. What did you ask me?"

"I asked if Lionel had phoned recently?"

"No, not since the first week when we blew the whistles each time he called."

"Why were you in such deep thought then?"

"I was thinking, how thankful I am, to be able to go to the park with Lucinda and find Audrey and Betty already there. Lucinda likes the park and the other children so much, and so do I. I practically do a five-mile run to get there. I am still afraid that Lionel will waylay me on the way to or from the park. But I do feel safe here with you."

"Do you still think Lionel is stocking you?"

"I don't know. Maybe it's me. I feel Lionel isn't ready to give up. He wants me back to be his frightened slave again. He felt that his home was his castle as long as I kept things meticulous. In contrast, I cowered in fear of his wrath if I didn't keep the house his way. I feel that he never loved me. He just liked to control me. That is what he is missing someone to control."

"Lucy, I have never told you, but I realized after Lucinda was born that I was living in fear all the time I was carrying her. I feared that I wouldn't be able to keep the house so meticulous and look after Lucinda the way I should in the first months of her life. I knew that would be a problem, which would provoke Lionel to be physically abusive. I would have lived in fear all the time."

"Oh, Diana, to think that someone could control your life to the extent that you would have to live in fear is terrible. You are certainly better off away from him. We will always help you to be free from him. I am sure Troy feels the same."

"Living here with you Lucy has helped. I don't think I could have stopped him if Lucinda and I had been on our own. The life of laughter and friendly atmosphere here has made my unbearable past life fade. I feel like a changed person living in the shared love, premating here, especially when you and Troy are together, and with your parents also. You always make me feel part of the family."

"That is easy because you have been family to us ever since you and Lucinda arrived on my doorstep. At the time, I needed you as much as you needed me. To my family's dismay, I wasn't getting over my grief the way I should have. So, I am thankful that you came, and Eric has completed the process. I guess you have figured that out." Lucy gave a chuckle and a slight blush at the thought of Eric and their last night together.

"Yes, but you had to stop your seminars. I feel bad about that. There is no way that my being here should interfere with your business."

"I'm enjoying the break. I will return to it as soon as I am sure Lionel is out of the picture, which seems to be the case now. If you are sure he has gone, I am thinking of one for a week from now, lasting three days." Lucy was thinking of Friday for the seminar and the weekend with Eric.

Diana was relieved that Lucy was going to give her seminars again. "I am sure Lionel has given up."

Lucinda called out in her baby language that she was awake. Diana went to get her. As she went upstairs, the fear that Lionel could show up was uppermost in her mind.

Lucy went back into her office. She made two phone calls. One to confirm that the scheduled seminar was still available. The other was to Eric confirming the weekend with him.

Lucy mentioned the crisis was over. Lionel was out of the picture for good. Eric was instantly making plans in his head for their weekend together. He was ready to ask Lucy to make a commitment to him. So, he wanted the weekend to be extra special."

Troy wasn't as sure as Lucy that Lionel was gone when he heard about the weekend seminar when Lucy called him to let him know her decision. It wasn't possible for him to be with Diana the whole time. But he would do his best.

He didn't want Lucy to give up her weekend because of Diana's situation. Something that may never happen. Besides, Diana was his responsibility. He was the one who coaxed Lucy to have Diana stay there.

He knew in his heart that he loved Diana and Lucinda. He wanted them to be his family. But he also knew that it wasn't possible while she was still married to Lionel. Diana was the type of person that would never have a casual affair. Besides, that wasn't what he wanted anyway. He wanted marriage, a wedding ring, and vows of love. Diana had too many principles for less than that which Troy respected.

Only once had divorce been mentioned. But Diana didn't feel Lionel would take that without some unpleasant reaction. So, Troy was sure she had discounted divorce as a means to get rid of Lionel.

Troy's difficulty was to be close to Diana, wanting to kiss her, and much more. But he had to make the best of this no-win situation. He had to be there for her safety while Lucy was away.

**

Diana wished there was some way she could be sure that Lionel had accepted that she was out of his life. Then she could tell Troy. The necessity would be gone for him to give up his weekend for her. Although, she was thinking about how much she enjoyed and wanted Troy in her life permanently.

She was having trouble hiding her jealousy of Lucinda and the attention he gave her when he held her and played with her. What kind of a mother was she that would be jealous of her baby? Diana wanted Troy to touch her and laugh with her too.

She shook her shoulders in open disgust at her inner thoughts of a love connection when she knew it was useless without freeing herself from her husband by divorce. Besides, Troy probably only thought of her as a sister anyway; she admonished herself. Either way, it was futile. But that is life. There are no guarantees. Life couldn't always work out the way we wish.

This weekend brought on thoughts of defeat and dread of Lionel bothering her.

Instead, she would rather enjoy the excitement of Lucy and Eric confessing their love for each other.

The weekend arrived, and Lionel had not contacted her.

Diana watched Lucy's excitement, wanting Lucy's happiness to be complete but dreading leaving if Lucy married.

Lucy had packed, unpacked, and repacked her wardrobe with seduction in mind. She could hardly contain her anticipation of the weekend ahead. Eric called every night, fearing each time that Lucy would say it was off because Lionel had reappeared.

Diana and Lucinda waved to her from the veranda. Lucinda had now learned to wave goodbye. Troy was instrumental in teaching her that. Otherwise, she had just fussed every time he left. This way, they had made a game of his leaving her.

Lucy wore a broad smile as she waved back. She drove away with the added hopes of defining her new path in life this weekend.

Diana got Lucinda ready for the walk to the park. The day was Friday, not knowing whether Audrey or Betty would be there. She arrived later because of Lucy's departure for the seminar and her romantic weekend.

Diana walked quickly. She kept up the chatter with Lucinda to cover her apprehension that her two friends hadn't come or had already left the park. Her qualms were ludicrous, believing that Lionel would waylay her. Lionel couldn't possibly know Lucy had gone away. Diana needed her friends around her to help dispel her fears.

As she went through the gate on the path to the swings and slides, she could easily see that her friends weren't there. Although there were several mothers and tots present, none were Betty or Audrey. Her steps faltered. Why was she scared? There were other people here. Undoubtedly, one of them would like to talk. Her firmer steps took her amongst the swings and slides.

Lucinda wanted a high swing. Then a slide. She couldn't climb the stairs, but Diana would place her partway up the slide, holding onto her, letting her slip down. So, she could giggle in delight. Lucinda's giggles rang out clearly in the morning air.

They were back at the swings. Diana was pushing Lucinda when male hands joined hers to give Lucinda a push. Diana froze. Blood rushed to her head as fear took over her body. She was so uptight that she could almost feel that she could break in half. Then a pleasant chuckle deflated her worries instantly. It was from Troy.

He was calling to Lucinda, "do you want to go higher?" Lucinda was trying to turn to see him and making noises. She wanted to go higher.

Diana was now enjoying his encasing arms protecting her, leaning back into him now that her fears had dispersed. They made a picture of a very loving, happily married couple with their baby. Both of them, reveling in the unexpected closeness that each of them had wanted so badly. Neither wanting to break the intimate embrace of this love-starved twosome, it was heaven.

All too soon, Lucinda indicated she had enough by raising herself, trying to remove herself from the swing.

Diana knew Lucinda wanted Troy to take her into his arms. But that meant Troy would release her. She was enjoying his embrace too much to break the link. The warmth of Troy's encircling arms around her had made a pulsating feeling of need throughout Diana's body.

Lucinda had one thought only now. She wanted Troy. He quickly went to catch her before she fell out of the offending swing that Lucinda no longer wanted. Troy was tickling Lucinda, making her giggle in between her slobbery kisses aimed at his face.

Diana's face mirrored her inner body glow from the embrace they had shared. Their first embrace was extraordinary. She studied Troy's face. There was no indication of how he felt about their shared embrace. She savored her happiness and enjoyed seeing her daughter, who was giggling with delight.

Diana chided herself. She mustn't build more into their embrace because it may not have been meant as love to him as it had to her.

Troy interrupted her thoughts. "Did you hear that Lucinda just called me Da? Isn't that wonderful?"

"But, Troy, you are not her Da," said Diana realistically.

"Yeah, but if Lucinda wants me to be her Da, that is alright with me." Troy kissed Lucinda on the cheek then rubbed his nose across her warm cheek to hear her giggles.

Now Diana had the memory of their hug locked into her heart, a sweet moment of closeness with Troy. Although, she felt now it wasn't an embrace on Troy's part.

"Are you ready to go now, Diana?" Troy's voice broke into her thoughts.

"Oh, oh, yes, we have been here a while." She faltered, remembering they had come later to the park because of Lucy's departure. But she wanted to leave anyway. As long as Lucinda had Troy's attention, she would like to go.

"Let's go." Troy put the happily squealing Lucinda into her stroller. Lucinda loved to have her legs unrestricted so she could move them freely. She was perpetually moving them.

Each day Diana and Lucinda spent time faithfully doing leg exercises. Diana prayed that Lucinda's legs would get more durable and straight. It was still too soon to tell until Lucinda started walking on her own. In the meantime, all she could do was hope.

When they arrived home, surprisingly, Troy broached the subject over coffee. "You know, Diana, it is time to have Lucinda's legs evaluated. She is pulling herself up more often, standing and stepping around furniture. So, it's only a matter of time before she will be walking. I think this is the perfect time to see Dr. Rushton. He has worked a lot with children with leg impediments. So, I think he would be the best one to give us his professional opinion on Lucinda's legs."

Diana's concern was instant. "I didn't think she would have a test this soon." As much as she wanted to know, she was afraid of the results.

"Diana, I want her legs to straighten naturally, too. But it is time. Her bones are fully developed now."

"Surely, she won't be walking for a couple of months. We do exercises daily."

"Diana, the exercise is to strengthen her legs. But it is the development of the bones that straighten the legs. I made an appointment with Dr. Rushton to see Lucinda next Tuesday." It was evident to his eyes that although Lucinda's legs had straightened a great deal. They were still not quite perfect.

"I have great respect for his work. You will like him. He specializes in these types of cases," said Troy, trying to alleviate some of Diana's concerns.

Diana's heart sank. She had not wanted Lucinda exposed to doctors. She had worked diligently, believing her legs would straighten on their own with exercises. Lucinda was so tiny. What would they do to her?

"Diana, I had hoped that you were prepared for this. I have mentioned this off and on over the months as Lucinda grew."

"Yes, but you said that they were getting straighter over time." Lucinda was hers to protect. She didn't want to submit Lucinda to testing.

Troy didn't want to expose her to testing either. But he knew it was time. Lucinda was as dear to him as she was to Diana. But he also knew that it was necessary. What he feared at her birth had come to pass. Her legs would need medical attention now for her to walk and run in the future. As a doctor, he knew Dr. Rushton would do the proper procedure on her so that she would be a potential star runner in the future. Troy had a lot of faith in Dr. Rushton.

Diana couldn't take it in. Why Tuesday? Why so soon?

"Can't we wait?" she pleaded.

"No, Diana, it should be done now. I have known for a month that this timing would be the best. I have brought it up on occasion, trying to prepare you for the necessity of medical attention."

"Yes, but with my worries about Lionel, I guess I wasn't taking it in properly. Troy, she is just a baby."

Troy reached across the table for Diana's hand, pushing aside her cup. "We will be together on this. I will make Dr. Rushton aware that I have an interest in this along with you. Diana, we have to do what is best for Lucinda now, not wait until too late. The care we take now may make the difference in a shorter period of medical treatment. Braces make the bones do what they need to for Lucinda's future to be normal."

"Braces?" Her eyes flew to Lucinda, playing cheerfully in her highchair, gumming a cookie. Her legs were moving along with her arms.

"I have mentioned braces before along the way. You have seen lots of children with braces on their teeth to straighten them. The principle is the same. It is only for a short period. Then they will no longer be necessary. But important for her when she starts walking."

Diana's eyes had swung to Troy. He could see her doubts and fears for Lucinda. He wanted to take it all away. But he had to be realistic. In his love for Lucinda, he knew she needed attention now.

He continued to squeeze Diana's hand gently, showing his love for her child. Both needed this touching to help alleviate their concern. But also, there was his unspoken love for Diana, which he hid because she was not free to accept his open love. It was impossible until she was free from Lionel. That was why he had never let himself show how he felt about her.

Lucinda took that moment to grab the cup from the table pushed in her direction. Their clinging hands broke apart. Troy reached for the falling cup, sending the forgotten cold tea onto the highchair tray and floor.

"Wow, little one, you are too young for tea yet." Lucinda's hand quickly moved to the brown liquid floating around on the highchair tray. Her tiny fingers were dipping into the brown liquid making the flow change direction towards herself. Diana jumped up to grab a dishcloth.

Troy held Lucinda's hands gently while Diana quickly made the brown liquid disappear. Troy put Lucinda's fingers in his mouth, gently sucking them to distract her, getting a taste of the mushy cookie. Lucinda giggled as Troy released her fingers.

"I think this young lady needs wiping off as well." He reached for the baby's cloth hanging nearby. He wet the facecloth to wipe Lucinda's hands and face after removing her bib. The offending crumbs of gooey cookies disappeared into the baby's washcloth. Then he picked her up to swing her around. Loving Lucinda, the way he wanted to love Diana.

The tension of the proposed doctor's visit was broken, but it still hung in the air.

Chapter Eleven

Diana was slowly coming to terms with the news that Troy had imparted. Of course, Lucinda needed to have another doctor's opinion. Why was she acting this way? Troy wouldn't recommend such a path if it wasn't necessary. If it meant braces, that would be what Lucinda would have to have. But where would she get the funds to buy them?

Lucy was paying her a nominal wage because their agreement included her room and board. Diana knew as Lucinda grew that larger braces would be required. She would just have to think about getting an evening job. Lucy could check on Lucinda as she went to bed early. She shouldn't be any bother.

What in the world could she do at night? Her minimal work experience didn't allow for much. Lionel had never wanted her to work, only to make his home into his castle of perfection as outlined for her in his schedule when they were first married.

Diana sighed. At least, she didn't have to keep to that plan anymore.

No one could help her get a job. Just be thankful you are out of the situation with Lionel, she chided herself. He would not have liked to buy Lucinda braces, even though Lionel's legs were not perfect anymore.

She just knew that she needed to start looking for a job. She had been putting it off far too long, living in this protective home.

It wasn't because of Lionel, that would only be a cop-out. It was because she liked the warm, happy atmosphere, cushioning her from reality. The reality was, she couldn't stay here forever. She had to make a life for herself and Lucinda. She knew that now more than ever because the weekends meant that Eric was in the picture, as far as Lucy was concerned. Soon there would be commitments between them.

Lucy had been too excited when she left just to be going to a seminar. Eric was definitely a part of her life. It was probably serious by now, judging from all his midnight calls. Oh yes, Diana heard them even if Lucy caught it after the first ring. So, it was only a matter of time before Lucy announced that she would be getting married.

Troy had enough of Diana's silence. Lucinda's legs had to be looked at professionally by an expert. He had delayed long enough, without telling her for this very reason. Was he wrong in not preparing her sooner?

"Diana, what are you thinking?"

"Troy, I accept Lucinda's legs need checking for their development. I was just trying to think about how I would pay for the doctor and the braces. I have been lax in letting the comfort of living here deter me from getting a proper job to support Lucinda and myself. Lucy has provided a warm, loving home for us. So, I never bothered to look for something that pays more. So that I could be independent and provide for Lucinda and my future."

"Isn't Lucy paying you enough beside your room and board? I know it is costly to rent and provide food along with daycare for Lucinda. This way, by working for Lucy, you can be with Lucinda daily. Rather than dragging her from babysitter to babysitter." Stressing that to make Diana realize that she had made the right choice. He didn't want her to have the complete burden of working to support Lucinda.

They would have less than the home she had here. It would probably come to that someday if she got looking for a job. He knew from their many talks that Diana didn't have much in the way of work experience. That was why this situation with Lucy had been so right for her.

Diana's mind was on the picture Troy had painted of dingy rooms and carrying Lucinda out half-awake, dragging her to a babysitter in the cold. Would the babysitter be as good with Lucinda as she would like? Now, she knew why she had never wanted to leave this homey atmosphere because the alternative was less than pleasant. Dingy rooms and babysitters did not inspire her to look for work. Her inexperience meant a job wouldn't be easy to find to support them.

"Diana, you aren't saying anything. Talk to me. What are you thinking?"

"Troy, I need to find a job to pay for the doctor and the braces. I should have looked for one long before now."

"But, Diana, you have liked being here. You have been happy, I know it. I will see if Lucy can increase your stipend. She seems to be doing well in her business now."

"Troy, that won't work. I am being paid well for what I do here. I only do housework and meals. Lucy is paying me well for what I do. I need a better-paying job if I am going to make any kind of life for Lucinda." She knew the time had finally come that she had to look for a job seriously.

"I have had my head buried in the sand far too long. It is this wonderful home, plus Lucy and the love that both of you have showered on Lucinda and me. But it is time to face reality. I can't evade it any longer. Lucy is ready to broaden her life's expectations now that she is completely over Mark and Connor's death. I know she is with Eric right now. I am sure he will be popping the question this weekend." She paused to let that sink in. Did he realize Eric and Lucy's relationship had reached that stage? Maybe Lucy wanted to tell Troy herself. What had she done, spouting off that way?

"Yes, I am aware that Lucy and Eric are together this weekend. I am also aware that they are serious about each other. I welcome it. I want Lucy to find happiness again. But I also know Lucy will take her time before she leaps into marriage," he said firmly. He didn't like the idea of Diana being out alone fending for herself. If only she were free to marry him. That set his heart beating faster at the thought.

"Troy, I think she will come home with the news that she is getting married. Eric isn't the type to want the current situation for too long. I think this is the weekend of truth. They have been parted more often since Lionel's attack, which dictated that Lucy stay home. I think he will spring the all-important question, maybe even as we speak. The midnight calls are a good indication of that."

"Midnight calls? You mean Eric phones here every night?"

"Oh yes, he rarely misses no matter where he is in the world. It must be difficult at times with the different time zones."

"Time difference shouldn't be much of a problem. He is on the San Diego to Honolulu run right now. At least, that is what he told me the last time he was here. He wanted a break from the long hauls for a while. To get his system back to normal, he said. Now come to think of it. He probably did it to be closer to Lucy."

"No doubt. Eric must hop a plane to Seattle with no difficulty when he is off duty. Lucy has been having a lot of seminars in Seattle and Portland. I noticed," offered Diana.

"So, it is more serious than I thought."

"Troy, she is more than ready for a new life. You need to realize that. Besides, you need to let go of your protective brother role. Lucy has recovered nicely from her sadness with Eric's help."

"I know. Just the loving brother instinct makes me think she still needs my brotherly love to bolster her. I have done it for so long it will be hard to let go."

"You know they won't want Lucinda and me around. Besides, Eric lives in San Diego. He will not want to commute forever. Lucy's business can flourish anywhere even if she moves there."

"Maybe, he could get transferred, basing him in Seattle. Maybe that is his intention if she says yes." Troy hated to think of Lucy being so far away as San Diego. They had too close a bond for that.

"Regardless, newlyweds aren't going to want Lucinda and me living here. They will want to be on their own."

Troy hadn't realistically thought of Lucy's private life, and he was unaware of the midnight calls until now.

His mind had been elsewhere. He had been concentrating on how he would broach Diana about Lucinda's doctor appointment for the past month.

Lucinda, who had been playing on the floor, decided it was time for attention. She crawled over to Troy to pull herself up. He helped her onto his lap, but he got a whiff of an odor.

"I think someone has been busy while we were talking," holding Lucinda out for Diana to take. She took Lucinda and her problem with her into the bedroom.

The latest dilemma of finding a job was hanging over her head. A new fear grew. How could she make a life away from Lucy and this loving home? Was she ready or capable of managing on her own?

When she went back into the kitchen, Troy was on the phone. Apparently, from the tail end of the conversation, he had made reservations for dinner at one of the local Inns.

She scolded him for making plans without consulting her. Troy reminded her that she would have said no as she usually did unless Lucy agreed to go with them.

"Okay, I'll go. How soon do I need to get us ready?"

"I made an early reservation because I am on duty tonight in the ER to attend to any children that may arrive or help out if there are major problems."

"We'd better get ready then." Diana went to get ready, taking Lucinda with her.

Troy went up to Lucinda's room with Diana. "I'll pick out something to dress her in after you wash her. Then you can get ready while I dress Lucinda," playing the role of the helpful daddy.

On exiting the bathroom, Diana handed over the happily squealing Lucinda to Troy. She wanted Troy whenever he was around. Diana went off to her bedroom as Troy talked to Lucinda while dressing her.

He talked about going to the Castleton Inn for dinner, mentioning foods that might tempt her. She had four teeth now, so she was able to eat most foods, even meat if it wasn't too chewy.

Diana was dressing with extra care. She didn't get many chances to dress up lately. They mainly had been eating at home. Her thoughts went back to her problem of getting a job.

What were her options? Maybe the Inn needed evening help. Waitressing or something like that. She would inquire when she was there. She didn't think Troy would mind.

They arrived at the Castleton Inn for their early dinner. The Maitre'd met them. "Good Evening, Dr. Sawyer. Your table is ready."

"Good evening, Albert."

"Right this way." Troy was carrying Lucinda as they followed the Maitre'd to their table.

Lucinda was craning her neck, trying to see all the people, and the lit candles on each table. Some patrons gave her an engaging smile as they passed. The dress Lucinda wore was a frilly pink dress that Troy had bought her. It enhanced her curly reddish-blond hair and pretty face. She looked like a little cherub. Lucinda returned the smiles with a charming smile of her own and her clutching wave.

The dinner tables were nearly full, which surprised Troy, as it was an early seating. He preferred to come around seven for a leisurely dinner, but circumstances would not allow that luxury tonight.

Troy had already arranged a highchair to be available. They were seated looking out onto the terrace, which had colorful fairy lights and a fountain in the courtyard.

"A new family, Dr. Sawyer?" Albert stepped back for Troy to seat himself.

"No, just friends of the family."

"Beautiful friends, I would say." Capturing Diana and Lucinda in a smile of approval for their beauty.

"Your waiter will be with you shortly. Tonight, it will be Thomas." He placed a menu before each of them. "Will you have a pre-dinner drink or just wine with your dinner?"

"Not tonight, Albert. I will be on duty this evening. Would you like something, Diana?"

"Not for me either, thank you." She smiled beguilingly at Albert.

"Well, enjoy your dinner. Don't work too hard tonight, Dr. Sawyer." Troy knew he meant he wished no catastrophic events for his ER duty tonight.

Troy's comment was, "yes. I hope it is a quiet night."

Thomas arrived while they were glancing at their menus. "Good evening, Dr. Sawyer. Good evening, madam. My name is Thomas. I am here to serve you tonight. The specials are a Seafood Flambe Stirfry or a Waldorf salad. The soup is Garden Ecstasy. I will give you a few more minutes for you to decide."

A young lad arrived with ice water and dinner rolls. He went over to Lucinda to tie a nylon bib with frolicking babies around Lucinda's neck to protect her pretty pink dress from spills. Lucinda loved everyone. She was craning her neck to pin the lad with her beguiling smile. The lad let out a laugh at her antics.

Troy was observing Diana, watching the exchanges between these young ones. He was mesmerized by her natural joy at seeing Lucinda so open with others. Troy wanted this lady to smile at him with the same ardor. She wasn't the type to be coy or pass feminine wiles about like some of his dates. Diana was unaware of her beauty, but he had indeed noticed her. Most of her beauty came from within.

"What would you like for dinner, Diana?"

"I don't know. I haven't quite previewed the menu," smiling directly at Troy.

"I thought I would have the Garden Ecstasy then the Beef Stroganoff in the white wine sauce," expressed Troy.

"That sounds good. But I'll have the Seafood Flambe Stirfry, and Lucinda prefers the chicken. She likes to gnaw on the bones. I brought a wet cloth in plastic to clean her after."

Thomas arrived to take their order. Troy ordered for them.

Diana added, "I will have earl grey tea served with my dinner after the soup."

Lucinda was awed by the colorful lights and fountain in the courtyard. The cascading water glimmered in a rainbow of colors from the fairy lights reflecting on the water. Troy and Diana were laughing at her wide eyes of wonderment at the display beyond the window.

During the dinner conversation, Diana was distracted, trying to think of how she could approach someone to see about a job without embarrassing Troy. After a superb dinner which they enjoyed, Diana excused herself. "Would you mind looking after Lucinda, please?"

"Not at all. Lucinda and I are great buddies, aren't we?" Tweaking Lucinda's cheek, which held gooey splatters from the chicken. She was still gnawing on a bone with glee.

Diana went to the front desk. She asked, "are there any openings for evenings that I can apply for?"

The young lady replied, "there is a waitress position for the dining room that is available, but I think they have enough applicants already."

Diana pleaded with the young lady to let her submit an application anyway. Annette gave in to her pleadings. Diana asked for a pen to fill it out right away. Annette indicated a little table near the desk to write on. Diana hoped she wouldn't take too long so that Troy came looking for her.

The Maitre'd observed Diana writing furiously at the small table. He went over to Annette to see if she knew what Diana was doing. He had noted Troy's concern at the length of time Diana was away from the table. Annette filled Albert in, "Diana is applying for the evening waitressing job." He tucked that away in his mind.

Diana arrived back at the table. "I'm sorry, Troy. I didn't mean to take so long."

"That's alright. Lucinda and I had dessert, which we both enjoyed. I didn't know if you wanted any. I didn't order any because you have never seemed to be big on desserts at home."

"That's fine. My dinner was more than enough for me." Hoping he wouldn't ask what took her so long.

"I washed Lucinda off after her chicken foray and the ice cream and cake that she was wearing. So, I think we are ready to go when we get the bill." He lifted his hand towards Thomas. Troy had prearranged that if he raised his hand, that meant Diana didn't require anything more. The dinner was over. The tally was to arrive immediately.

Diana was putting on Lucinda's coat in the foyer where they had left their coats. Troy attended to their bill. He arrived in time to help Diana into hers.

Lucinda was hammering with her hand on the padded chair, liking how her hand bounced off the cushion. She was busily talking to the seat. Lucinda loved to stand now, holding on to furniture.

Diana was anxious to leave before anyone said anything to her about her application. Troy picked up Lucinda, following the hurrying figure of Diana, who was speedily exiting the door.

Then she heard a voice calling Troy. It sounded like Albert.

"Dr. Sawyer. Dr. Sawyer. Wait."

Diana had almost made her escape. Sure enough, the Maitre'd caught up to them. Diana thought he was going to say something to Troy about her job application. Just a few seconds more, and they would have been in the car.

"What is it, Albert?"

"Dr. Sawyer, you left your credit card in the tray when you paid your bill." Albert was extending his fingers, holding the credit card. Diana breathed a sigh of relief. Then Albert gave her a knowing look. Here it comes. He is going to say something. Instead, Albert wished them both a good evening then turned to walk back into the Inn.

"I must be losing it. That is the first time I have ever misplaced a credit card."

Diana was once again heading for the car. She didn't want Troy to see her face, expressing her relief at making a safe getaway.

"Diana, what is your hurry?"

"You have to go to work, don't you? Besides, I need to get Lucinda ready for bed soon." She was beside the car waiting. She needed Troy to open the door so that she could find sanctuary in the car's dark interior.

Troy flicked the gizmo on his key chain. The locks flipped open. Diana pulled open the door before Troy could reach her. She stuck her head into the car to fiddle with the belts on Lucinda's car seat in preparation for strapping her in for the ride home.

Troy mentioned, "I'll put her in Diana." She stepped aside but was unable to reach the passenger door because of Troy's body.

Lucinda was safely secured. He stepped back to close the door, placing his hand on the door handle of the front seat. Gallantly opening the door for Diana to ease inside. He bent in over her. "Do you want me to buckle you in too?" Whipping the seat belt around the circle of her body before she could grab the belt.

His face brushed her cheek as he securely attached the buckle. Their eyes made contact. There had been a tingle from his touch. Troy stood suspended for a moment before he pulled back to close the door.

Diana brushed her hand across her cheek, aware of the tingle. Troy circled the front of the car to the driver's side. Diana quickly clamped her hands together in her lap so that Troy couldn't see her reaction to their contact with each other.

"All set to go?" Troy asked as he turned on the ignition.

"Troy, I want to thank you for taking Lucinda and me for dinner. The dinner was delicious. Lucinda enjoyed her dinner too."

Lucinda's started her baby talk in response to her name.

"You're both welcome," replied Troy.

"Troy, I know I gave you a hard time when you mentioned the doctor's appointment for Lucinda. You had indicated there was a chance her legs could straighten, and I had hoped she would do it on her own. I am sorry I gave you a hard time about it. But I was taken by surprise. Of course, something as serious as her legs needs checking. Thank you for arranging it."

He wanted her to be accepting. But he also had tried to shield her from the specialist visit for as long as possible.

"I understand," he said as if it was no big deal, being nonchalant as possible.

"You have always been there for Lucinda and me. How could I have reprimanded you the way I did upon hearing the news about the dreaded appointment. You have always been there for me. You are so thoughtful and kind. What did I do but give you a hard time? I am sorry."

Diana was studying his profile. He was such a nice man, caring, straightforward, and loving to Lucinda. She wished Troy would include her in the loving like a woman needed to be loved. He was not her brother. In all honesty, she wanted Troy as a man.

He could feel her eyes on him studying him. Why? *Could she be noticing him at last? He certainly hoped so.* His eyes slipped off the road to meld with hers.

Could he see the desire in her eyes?

He broke the contact quickly to observe the route ahead. For safety, or was he afraid to see the truth in her eyes, that she was only thankful for his concern for Lucinda's wellbeing.

Chapter Twelve

They arrived home from the Inn. "I need to leave immediately. I will help you in with Lucinda then leave."

"I can manage Lucinda. You should be on your way,"

Troy was out of the car before she could entirely free herself from her belt. He had the back door open. He was surprised to see Lucinda's eyes open. She had been so quiet. He thought she had fallen asleep.

"Da, Da." Lucinda put her face against his for a kiss. Her little arms encircled his neck. The imp had learned this was the way of getting his full attention.

Troy was immensely proud to be recognized as 'dada' by her, even if it wasn't entirely true. He gave her a loving kiss on the cheek, squeezing her a little. She giggled.

"You are a charming minx. Do you know that?"

When Troy tried to release her amongst her giggles, she held on, not wanting him to leave. "All right, I will carry you inside, but I have to go."

"Da, Da." Troy enjoyed the fallacy as he felt like a daddy to her.

"Troy, I can take her. Thank you for the wonderful dinner." Diana wanted him gone before he picked up on the vibes of her need for him. She was sure the message was in her eyes.

"Okay and your welcome." He tried to release Lucinda's encircling arms. She was holding on tightly. A position Diana wanted with him.

"One more kiss, then you have to go to your mommy." Troy gave Lucinda another kiss then propelled her body towards Diana. But the way her arms still clung, she brought his head forward, and as Diana leaned forward to pick Lucinda out of his arms, their lips accidentally came in contact. Somehow neither could break away. A mewing noise of invitation came from Diana. Troy increased the melding of their lips.

Lucinda's arms tried to encircle them both. Her arms tightened on them, kissing first Diana, then Troy, joining in the fun of clinging lips. They were powerless to break the spell they were both under. Diana felt bereft as Troy managed to pull away against his will. "Goodnight, Diana. Sweet dreams," pulling Lucinda's arms away.

"Goodnight, Troy," Diana whispered. She savored their first kiss.

Lucinda was waving bye, bye to Troy, who was standing by his car. Troy got into the car and drove away. A bit of Diana's heart went with him.

Diana walked to the door light-hearted. Then inside, she felt her foot kick something.

She put Lucinda down on the hall chair to remove her coat. Then she stood Lucinda up, holding onto the chair. Diana reached for the paper she had kicked with her foot.

When she read it, she felt like a glass of ice water had been thrown into her face. A quick jolt from ecstasy to instant fear.

Diana

You are my wife. I intend to have you back with me. Be sure you are aware I am coming for you. I watch you constantly.

Lionel

The fear she felt erased all the tender feelings of Troy's kiss. The nightmare was back. Lionel wasn't about to give up. If only there hadn't been a letter slot for him to leave his message. She crushed the letter, and the tears began. How could she stop him? She was powerless to do so.

She picked up Lucinda, and her little arms went around Diana's neck, reigning kisses on her cheeks as she carried her to the bedroom. Her unhappy mother sank sadly into the rocker in

Lucinda's room. The tears rained unchecked, and hopelessness invaded her mind. Lucinda started to cry, sharing her mother's grief.

Diana didn't know how long she had been grieving. She felt so drained of life. Diana got up like a robot. She had cried herself into numbness, letting her fear of Lionel take over her mind.

She went through the motions of getting Lucinda ready for bed. The frightened Lucinda fought against getting undressed and getting her pajamas on. She was irritable and rebellious. Diana didn't seem to notice. Her fingers and hands moved, but her mind was closed in her despair.

Lucinda was so tired after her defiance that she fell asleep as soon as her head hit the pillow.

Diana walked down the hall to her room. Unmindful of her attire, she curled into a ball under the covers. Sleep eventually released her from reality.

Lucinda's crying awoke her. Diana sprang up only to fall back onto the pillow. She had a violent headache. It was then she realized that she had her clothes on. What happened to her? The horrible memory of the message burst into her mind. What was she going to do?

Lucinda was wailing now. Diana had to get up. She had to go to Lucinda when all she wanted to do was curl up into a ball again, obtaining oblivion. Her head was pounding with hammers of pain. She had to get up to attend to her crying baby. She listened. That is strange Lucinda was quiet. Had she gone back to sleep?

Diana closed her eyes, hoping she was dreaming.

When a voice said, "Diana, what happened? I tried knocking, but I got no answer, so I opened the door in fear that there was something wrong. What in the world is the matter?"

Diane's eyes flew open. Troy was holding Lucinda. Diana rolled over to hide her face in the pillow.

Troy put Lucinda down on the bed. He pulled the covers away from Diana then sat down beside her. He picked her up in his arms. She came willingly. "Oh, Troy. I am faced with Lionel again. I don't know what to do?"

"What do you mean faced with Lionel? I don't understand."

"When I opened the door last night, there was a letter from Lionel."

"What did it say?"

She burrowed into Troy's shoulder, and Lucinda tried to pull herself up on Troy's arm. In her muffled voice, Diana said, "he is still coming for me. He said he watches me all the time." She moaned as another stab of pain pierced her head.

"He will not get you. Now, we have to get you out of these clothes. Then get you dressed. I'll make the coffee and breakfast. We'll talk about this later." Lucinda was standing, trying to get on his lap, which Diana was filling.

"Lucinda, not now, honey. Mommy needs some attention." Troy pushed her down gently. He laid Diana back down on the pillows. His hands were undoing the tiny buttons of her lacy top that had made her look so feminine at dinner last night.

It must have sunk in what he was doing. Diana's hands came up to stop him. Her hands covered his. Troy's hands that had been impersonal were trapped against her breast under Diana's modest seeking hands.

Troy knew this was not the time for this type of contact. He gently extracted his hands from where Diana's hands had imprisoned his.

Troy's hands were gone. He was saying, "Diana, you have to get undressed. You can't stay in those clothes. You slept in them all night." Troy's voice was gruff with emotion. He was having difficulty curbing his feelings. The last thing Diana needed right now was a sex-craved man.

"Lucinda, you sit there until I get back. Don't get off the bed," he said firmly. He pulled Diana up, helping her into the bathroom. "I'll bring you some clothes."

Lucinda's little lips quivered. She didn't understand. What was the matter with her mommy? She was acting strange, and so was dada. But she plunked down on her bottom and stopped her crawling.

Troy was back, glancing at Lucinda. Sadly, she was sitting, waiting for attention.

"Uncle Troy will be with you in a minute. I just need to get your mommy some clothes, grabbing a sweater, jeans and underwear from her drawers. He hoped this was an okay outfit. He didn't think that they had time to be fussy.

He needed to attend to Lucinda before she fell off the bed. He whipped her up in passing, heading to the bathroom. He knocked. Then he opened the door enough to shove the clothes inside with his extended arm, waiting for her to take them. The clothes disappeared from his hand. He pulled his hand back out and closed the door saying, "don't be too long. I am getting breakfast ready."

"Come on, pumpkin. We are going to make breakfast for your mommy." He headed downstairs. He put Lucinda in her chair and tied a bib on her. Then gave her an Arrowroot cookie to munch.

He whizzed around the kitchen, all the while keeping up a conversation with Lucinda and receiving baby talk replies.

Coffee was his prime aim first, then an omelet. Diana arrived as he flipped the cheese and mushroom omelet on three plates from the big skillet he held easily in his hand.

"Coffee is coming after the omelet is on the table," he said casually.

Diana sat down. Her head fell into her raised hands. She was waiting for the aspirins to kick in, to remove her slicing headache.

"Diana, do you have a headache?"

"Yes, but I took some aspirin. I am just waiting for the pills to work. I don't want breakfast, just coffee."

"What? You don't want to taste my masterpiece. I am offended. You have to eat it all before we discuss Lionel," placing a plate in front of her. The omelet did look very tempting. But she wasn't sure she could enjoy it until her headache receded.

Troy took a fork full. "Hmm, perfection, come on, Diana, try some. Even Lucinda is showing approval."

Lucinda spread more omelet on her tray than into her mouth as she dug in with her fingers ignoring her spoon. But what she managed to keep in her mouth, she ate with gusto.

"Try some, Diana." Troy held his fork up to Diana's obediently opening mouth to the tasty egg omelet.

Due to the aspirin kicking in, she was able to savor her next fork full. Troy was pleased that she picked up her fork and started eating. It was a good sign.

He wouldn't discuss Lionel until breakfast was over and the dishes were washed. Troy was examining all their options in his head with this delaying tactic. Police protection was out. Staying in the house unless someone was with her was not acceptable. Moving away from town, no, he didn't want that. Should he ask her to live with him? Would that stop Lionel? No, Diana wouldn't go for that. When all was said and done, there weren't many options.

After breakfast, they moved into the living room so Lucinda could play within their eyesight while they talked.

"Diana, can I see Lionel's note?"

"I screwed it up and threw it away. Lionel's note said he still intended to have me for his wife and that he was watching me."

"I gave it considerable thought. Do you think that if someone else had you with them, then Lionel might give up?"

"What do you mean if someone else had me?"

"I mean, what if you live together with a male? Would that make a difference to him?"

"But I don't know any men. I don't know if it would make a difference. I can't believe Lionel is doing this. I can't believe he would not acknowledge his baby either. I just don't know him anymore," her voice trailed off in despair.

Troy wanted to pull her into his arms to comfort her, but he needed a clear head to resolve the problem.

"Lucy could stay home more."

"Troy, I will not make Lucy stay home for me. I will not make Lucy a prisoner in her own home. Especially not now that she has Eric in her life. I wouldn't mind betting Eric is proposing to her this weekend. She was so excited about her trip. It had to be Eric that was making her glow when she left."

"I think you are right. Lucy may come home with a ring on her finger."

He reached for Diana's hand. "Diana, when I said if you were to cohabit with a male, I meant me. I want you and Lucinda to come and live with me." At Diana's look of shock, he quickly added, "it would be platonic, but Lionel wouldn't have to know that."

"But Troy, I am married. I can't live with you."

"I said platonically, that means separate bedrooms. I just want to protect you and Lucinda."

"I don't think that is wise." Diana wished she could say yes, despite her answer.

"Diana, please just think about the possibility. I have thought and thought this out. That is all I can come up with that might deter him."

"Okay, but until Lucy says otherwise, I think it is best that I stay here."

Lucinda decided she wanted her dada's attention. She pulled herself up on Troy's pant leg. He quickly picked her up and placed her on his knee. Then he claimed Diana's hand. She was looking down at their joined hands as though it was a new experience. Her fingers intertwined with his. It felt good to have the contact. Things always felt better when Troy was around.

Troy thought it best to drop the subject for now. "Let's take Lucinda to the park. It is a nice day. We all need some fresh air." He arose, with Lucinda in his arm. He didn't release Diana but pulled her up with him.

"All right," said Diana wanting the conversation to end for now.

Troy was pushing Lucinda in her stroller, and Diana walked close by his side as they left the house. They made the picture of the perfect loving couple. Lionel was seething as he watched them walk down the street. He was in a van with tinted windows. He could see them, but they couldn't see him.

Diana was getting entirely too friendly with Dr. Sawyer. He would have to claim his wife very soon. "That is quite the family picture, well Diana, there'll be no divorce," he ranted out loud.

Lionel started the engine. He zoomed away from the curb, and in his anger, Lionel's foot tromped on the gas, making the car swerve towards the curb just as he passed them. Then he whipped it back into the road properly.

Troy and Diana stopped in horror, realizing their brush with near-death as the van sped away. Troy noted the license, but he didn't tell Diana. He had a good memory for numbers. He could undoubtedly remember that one as it ended in DYE.

"Wow, that was too close for comfort. Whoever that was, drove like a maniac. We were lucky that they managed to get back under control." Diana was staring after the van.

"Yes, that was too close for comfort. They should have their license taken away." Lionel's name popped into Troy's mind. But he didn't let on to Diana.

When they got to the park, Troy tried to make Diana forget the near-death experience. He had Lucinda laughing with his antics of pretending to be a monkey on the monkey bars, causing Diana to smile.

Audrey happened by. Diana introduced her to Troy. He encouraged Diana to talk with Audrey while he gave Lucinda another swing before they headed home.

After Audrey revealed Betty went to her mother-in-law's place for the day, Diana mentioned the incident with the van going out of control, which had endangered their lives. Audrey knew about Lionel as Diana had confided in her one day. During the time when Lionel was harassing her by phone. "Do you think it was Lionel?" asked Audrey.

"No. Because of the tinted windows, I couldn't see in, but I hope not." Now that she was talking about it openly with Audrey, the more reasonable it sounded like it was him, after all. He must have a new car. Surely, he wouldn't kill them in broad daylight? No, he said, he wanted her back. Why would he kill her if that was the case?

"You know, Diana, the tinted glass does sound like someone could easily hide behind it. I would go to the police to report this incident if I were you. They should know for future reference if anything more happens."

"That is the reason why Troy is with me. Lucy had to go away for the weekend. Troy didn't want me to be by myself because of Lionel. Now it would seem to be for a good reason."

Audrey looked over at the swings. "Yes, it does. Troy really loves Lucinda, doesn't he?"

"Yes, they have developed quite a bond between them. She is going to miss him when we have to leave Lucy's place."

"Leave? Are you leaving Lucy's?"

"Yes, maybe. Lucy may be announcing that she is marrying Eric soon. I know she was so excited about going away. No seminar makes a person that happy. I can't stay at her place once she marries. Besides, Eric lives somewhere else, and he will surely want her with him."

"I'm sorry to hear that. This arrangement was so perfect for you. When will this happen?" Audrey inquired.

"I don't know. But I will have to get a job of some kind to support Lucinda and me. Even if I stay, I would have to get a job. Lucinda is having her legs tested on Tuesday. Troy has been preparing me in case she needs braces to correct her leg structure."

"Oh, Diana, that on top of Lionel too. I wish I could help." Audrey knew the cost of specialists and braces must be too high for Diana, especially in her present situation. "What type of job will you look for?"

Diana looked over at Troy. He was pushing Lucinda on the swing, much to Lucinda's delight.

"I applied at the Castleton Inn last night for night waitressing so Lucy could watch Lucinda. But I doubt I will get the job. The girl who took my application said they already had many applicants, and I have no experience."

"You never know. Sometimes you are chosen because of your name, or you were the applicant that appealed to them for some reason that can't be defined." Audrey knew she was being a bit farfetched. But she felt sorry for Diana. She really liked her.

Cowan got up from the sandbox and came over to them. He wanted to go home. So, Audrey and Diana said their goodbyes.

Diana walked towards Troy, who was removing Lucinda from the swing. He watched Diana's face as they walked towards each other. He had hoped that talking to her friend would take away some of her worries. But by the look of it, there was more worry on her face. She came closer, pushing the stroller. Obviously, Audrey and Diana had not just had an idle conversation. She must have confided in her friend.

"All set to go?" asked Troy.

"Yes, we should get Lucinda home. She will be tired after being here so long. Besides, aren't you hungry?"

"Yes, Diana. I fancy a hamburger. How about we go to Burger Baron on the way home. Their hamburgers taste scrumptious. They are big and juicy."

"Yes, that might be a good idea. We can sit at the tables outside."

Troy put Lucinda in the stroller. He started pushing her. Troy wanted to pull Diana up against his side to reassure her that things would be all right. But he wasn't sure how she would respond or if he could really make it all right.

If only he could take control of her protection, maybe that would help. Troy was sure the van had belonged to Lionel. He would give the police the license number 786DYE for them to check. Hopefully, they would be able to tell him.

They arrived at Burger Baron. The young fellow there took a shine to Lucinda. So, he fixed up a special dinner for her. It was a pattie cut in tiny bite-size pieces with gravy drizzled over them and some mashed potato. For Troy and Diana, he made the Baron Burger's Special Deluxe Hamburger.

When Diana saw the size of it, she protested. The young man said, "they are so delicious the way I make them. I guarantee you won't want to stop eating until it's all gone," he said with a cheery smile.

They made their way to an outside table, choosing one at the back with additional stroller space. Troy went to get a highchair for Lucinda.

Troy placed the hamburgers on the table and Lucinda's special meal. Then he took their drinks from the tray, Pepsi for himself, iced tea for Diana, and Lucinda's milk. Lucinda was trying to use a cup now. Some of it went down the front of her.

The young man's words were valid. Once Diana started eating, she soon finished her hamburger, enjoying every morsel. But the fries were too many until Troy helped her with them.

Troy was waiting for Diana to finish her iced tea. He needed to protect her. He wanted to make a proposal that he hoped she would accept.

"Diana, I feel the same as you. I think Lucy will be making an announcement after her weekend with Eric. If there is an immediate change to her living arrangement, like moving to Eric's place, I want you to come and live with me. I don't think you should be living alone. Not with Lionel's threats hanging over you. It would be a platonic relationship. You'll have your own bedroom and so will Lucinda. I need to be in the picture to protect you. Do you understand what I'm saying?"

"Yes, Troy, but I can't do that. Again, it would only be temporary until you meet someone important to you, if you haven't already. Then you, too, will be asking me to leave. No, if Lucy leaves, I will get a place of my own." Her chin was very determined.

Chapter Thirteen

The rest of the weekend passed with no further incident, and Diana's leaving Lucy's place was a closed subject.

Lucy arrived home with a happy air about her. Obviously, her weekend had lived up to her expectations. Although Lucy never mentioned that she and Eric had any immediate plans, so Diana was safe with their living arrangements for a while yet.

Tuesday dawned with the knowledge that this was the day of Lucinda's specialist appointment. Troy was coming at ten to take them to see the doctor. Diana and Lucinda were all ready to go when he arrived.

Troy greeted Lucy with a kiss. "Catch you later to ask about your weekend as we have to go now."

Turning, he asked, "are you ready?" Diana indicated yes. Lucy wished them good luck and good news.

Troy picked up Lucinda. Diana preceded them out with a diaper bag and her purse. When they were all strapped in, Troy drove to the medical building on Skylar Street. Diana wanted Lucy's wish for good news to be the same as Troy's prediction of righting itself as her bones developed. But deep down, she knew it wouldn't be that simple.

Lucinda played with the toys in the waiting room corner, providing entertainment for the other waiting children.

When it was Lucinda's turn, Troy went in with them. He greeted Dr. Rushton by his first name. He had gone to medical school with him. "Hello, Neil. This young lady is Lucinda. Her mother is Diana Cardwell."

"Hello, Troy. Nice to see you again. My, these ladies with you are certainly very pretty." Diana blushed at his comment.

"Why don't we head into the examining room. I want to take some X-rays after."

They went into the adjoining room. Dr. Rushton took Lucinda from Troy and laid her down on the examining table, moving her legs in several ways to see how they responded to different positions. He sat her up and checked her reflexes. Then he stood her up. Lucinda was smiling at Troy, who was standing to the right of them.

"So, you have an eye for the good doctor, do you, little one?" Dr. Rushton glanced over at Troy. "So, Troy has used his charm on you, has he?"

"You have it wrong, Dr. Rushton," said Diana. "Lucinda charmed him. I think that is more like it."

"Then he is a lucky man. Wouldn't you say, Troy?"

"Yes, she definitely charmed me. But it wasn't difficult to surrender to her charisma," replied Troy.

All the while they were talking, Dr. Rushton had been holding onto Lucinda while she walked back and forth on the examining table. Lucinda loved to walk. So, she was cooperating. She wasn't making shy either. Perhaps because of the friendliness between the two men.

"Troy, would you mind accompanying me to the X-ray room? So, Lucinda doesn't get scared. Mrs. Cardwell, would you like to wait in my office? We won't take long."

Diana headed back into Dr. Rushton's office. She was glad she didn't have to watch those big machines hovering over her daughter's legs.

"How are things going, Troy?" Dr. Rushton inquired as they walked along.

"Fine. I think I should tell you I have a special interest in Lucinda."

"Yes, I got that impression. It is more than a doctor and patient relationship."

"Yes. Diana and Lucinda live with my sister. I know them well as I visit them often. They are very special to me."

“So, they live with your sister, Lucy, wasn’t it? I remember meeting her at our graduation. I always wanted to ask her out on a date. Somehow, the occasion never came up. I don’t know why when I think back now.”

“That’s funny because she once said she would like to meet you socially. She used to bug me to call you. But I thought you were dating at the time.”

“I was but nothing serious. Oh well. Is Lucy married?”

“No, but soon I think.”

“That’s life.” He smiled as they entered the X-ray room.

Troy carried Lucinda over to the machine gurney. He set her down to remove her shoes and socks. Troy caressed Lucinda’s cheek with his finger so she wouldn’t be frightened while Dr. Rushton set her legs in the position to be X-rayed.

“Troy, I think there is more attachment between you and Lucinda than just living at your sister’s.”

“Yes, there is. That is why I am here with them. I have a vested interest in Lucinda. I would like to marry her mother and have Lucinda as my daughter.”

“I thought so. When is the big day?”

“No big day. Diana is married. Separated but married. Diana won’t consider my feelings as long as she is married. So, I haven’t spoken about my feelings as of yet.”

“I’m sorry to hear that. You looked like the perfect family when I first saw you enter my office. Too bad.”

“From what you have seen so far, what do you think?” Troy was curious.

“These X-rays should make it clear. But from what I have already observed. I will say that she needs braces unless the X-rays show more. I think that an operation is unnecessary. But we’ll have to wait for the actual X-rays before I can say for sure. Let’s go back to Mrs. Cardwell while we wait.”

Troy redressed Lucinda, and they headed back to Diana. Lucinda was giving Troy loving kisses as they walked. Dr. Rushton was laughing. “You, young lady, are a flirt.”

Lucinda giggled as if she knew what he was saying.

Troy sat down beside Diana with Lucinda on his lap. He grasped Diana’s hand to reassure her. He had noticed her anxious look as they entered.

Dr. Rushton sat behind his desk. “The nurse will be bringing the X-rays in shortly. In the meantime, can you tell me a bit about her legs? The things you have noticed as she has grown so far, Mrs. Cardwell?”

“Her legs have straightened considerably as her bones have developed. But it appears not enough, according to Troy. I have been doing exercises daily to strengthen her legs as I thought that might help. I had hoped her bones would continue to straighten so that braces wouldn’t be necessary.” The cautious way she made the last comment made Dr. Rushton realize Diana didn’t want Lucinda to have braces.

Before he could answer, the nurse arrived with the X-rays. “Mrs. Cardwell, would you excuse Troy and me while we look at the results?”

She murmured, “not at all.” Troy handed Lucinda to Diana.

Troy followed Neil into the examining room, where they put the X-rays on the lit viewing screen. The X-rays clearly showed the bones needed more straightening. “Braces should be enough.”

Troy sighed in relief.

“From your sigh, I take it you think braces might do the trick. I am glad Lucinda’s bones have straightened as they developed. I don’t like to operate on someone so young. I would say she is a lucky girl not needing an operation, after all. Continuing with the braces as she grows should complete the straightening. Well, let’s get back to Mrs. Cardwell. She will be getting anxious.”

Lucinda held out her arms to Troy. He automatically eased her off Diana’s lap and onto his. He reached out for Diana’s hand, squeezing it. Troy was smiling, so Diana let out the breath she was holding.”

Dr. Rushton proceeded, “when I first saw Lucinda’s baby X-rays, I thought she would need an operation. But miraculously, her legs have straightened as her bones developed. But I feel they need more help now that she is standing and will soon be walking. Therefore, I am recommending braces.”

Diana’s face fell enough for them to know that she hoped that braces wouldn’t be necessary.

"Mrs. Cardwell, if she has braces now for her legs, she will discard them before she is a teenager, or even much sooner."

Diane's eyes flew to Troy. She didn't want to let Dr. Rushton know her disappointment was partly caused by her inability to afford the necessary braces as she had no Medical Insurance.

Troy squeezed her hand. "Diana, it won't be so bad. Lucinda will adjust to them easily. She is a determined little girl."

Troy did not pick up on Diana's reason for concern. She gave him a weak smile, more like a recoil. Nobody is discussing the cost of braces, but she couldn't form the words to ask.

Lucinda took that moment to want to go back to Diana. Maybe, Lucinda realized her mother's reserve. Diana took the time to compose her thoughts. Could she handle the expense? Were they costly? Why were they not revealing any cost?

When Diana had settled Lucinda on her knee, she had composed her facial expression to hide her misgivings.

Dr. Rushton felt terrible for this woman, even though he didn't know all of Diana's circumstances but guessed there might be money issues. Troy had told him to say that the braces would be a gift from a local fund-raising organization. Not looking at Troy, he started in on his spiel.

"Mrs. Cardwell, now that I have told you about Lucinda's need for braces. I want to mention a local organization that does all manner of generous donations to children with physical problems. They have set up a special fund for children like Lucinda. You won't need to pay for them. I will measure Lucinda to order the braces for her legs. She will start wearing them when she starts to walk." Diana's face had broken out into a smile of relief.

"How can that be? Really, do people donate things like that?"

"Oh, yes. Our community is good at helping people, be it children or otherwise."

Troy had privately indicated that the bill was to come to him for the braces. Troy didn't want Diana to know because she wouldn't take charity from him.

"I am thankful. I was wondering how I would be able to pay for the braces. I am sure that they are expensive." She hugged Lucinda. Thankful to hear that she will get the help she needs.

Dr. Rushton didn't go into the cost. He didn't want to get in any deeper. So, he changed the conversation to the use of the braces instead. "Lucinda will have to come in for regular check-ups as she grows and for replacement braces as required. Do you and Troy want to wait here while my nurse and I do the measuring? She doesn't seem to be making strange at all." The nurse took Lucinda from Diana. Lucinda looked doubtful, but the nurse started talking to her. Lucinda seemed to be interested in what she had to say.

Diana looked at Troy. "I can't believe that organizations do things like donating braces. I have never heard of that before. Is there someone I can speak to? I want to thank them."

"Diana, these organizations do this all the time. They never expect nor want thanks. They just want to help children have a better quality of life." Troy tried diverting her. "Lucinda is very cooperative with the nurse and Neil. I thought she might make strange."

"Lucinda has a friendly nature. The only thing she picked up on was my concern. I was dreading the cost to pay for them."

"I thought you were. I should have mentioned the chance that this organization would be willing to help. I am familiar with their generous donations. Then you wouldn't have been needlessly worried."

"Troy, will it hurt Lucinda to wear these braces?"

"No, she will be stiff-legged in the way she walks. But she will get used to them in time. Crawling will be quite a bit different for her, especially from what she has been doing now. You will have to spend more time with her until she gets used to them. So she doesn't hurt herself unnecessarily."

Dr. Rushton came back carrying Lucinda. She was tugging on his beard. "You know, young lady, that is attached to me. So, go easy with that." He had a big grin. He was not upset at all.

Diana was thankful for his pleasantness after seeing what Lucinda was doing. She was sure Dr. Rushton was the first man with a beard that Lucinda had met.

"All done. Lucinda was perfect through it all. No complaints from her."

Troy reached up to take her.

"The braces should be in next Thursday. So, set up an appointment for Lucinda to be fitted."

They stood up, both thanking Dr. Rushton for his help. Diane specified, "Thursday was fine. I will check with the nurse for a time."

**

Diana put the braces on for a couple of hours each day at Dr. Rushton's suggestion, acclimatizing Lucinda to wearing them. She felt sorry for Lucinda as the braces hampered her quick crawl. The sound of the braces scraping the floor made Lucinda stop.

Dr. Rushton had indicated that the supports wouldn't hurt her. The strangeness of them was receding, and Lucinda stopped protesting. But Diana figured it would be only a matter of time before Lucinda would realize that they would be part of her legs from now on. She did not like the hampered crawling that slowed her down considerably.

Diana worried that the braces might leave scratch marks on the floor.

Lucy said, "Don't worry about that. I just don't like to see her tiny legs encased in the steel." Her heart went out to Lucinda. But she knew that they were necessary for Lucinda to walk correctly in the future.

Diana made two hours each day for Lucinda's standing and walking time in braces. She firmly believed the braces hurt her when she crawled unless she was on the deep pile rug in the living room.

Lucinda was getting the idea to hold onto the furniture to move around and walk. Diana wondered if Lucinda realized that her mother never encouraged her to walk unless she had the braces on.

During this period of adjustment, Lucy and Troy were supportive, encouraging both Diana and Lucinda.

At first, Diana wouldn't put them on if she was taking Lucinda out elsewhere. She just carried her all the time. But now, Lucinda wanted to stand and try to walk, making her restless in Diana's arms. Making it more difficult to restrain her, tiring Diana. She knew that she would have to increase Lucinda's time in braces. She was ready to walk.

Chapter Fourteen

Diana, amazingly enough, had been hired by the Castleton Inn to waitress evenings. She felt sure that Albert the Maitre'd was responsible for her hiring. She had no qualifications in waitressing. Diana learned quickly and became popular with the clientele because of her sweet manner.

Lucy was happy for her. Diana always made sure that Lucinda had her bath and was in her pajamas before she left. So, Lucy just had to feed her and put her to bed.

Troy had not taken the news lightly. After working around the house all day and attending to Lucinda, she would be too tired to toil on her feet all evening. But of course, he never said that. Diana needed this to be more independent. His misgivings were that Lionel would find out. Troy now knew the van was registered to Lionel that had almost mowed them down. But he never saw the auto near the house again, but he still felt he was around somewhere.

Troy was afraid Lionel was going to abduct her on the way to or from the Inn somehow. He didn't want her to become paranoid. So, he deliberately did not mention this to her.

Diana served drinks in the lounge a few nights when they weren't busy in the dining room. But being new, Diana knew, she hadn't much choice. She preferred the dining room and its gracious patrons.

She wasn't comfortable when some men had a few drinks. They were inclined to ogle her or touch her. She didn't have the natural manner of laughing it off. She just withdrew. Anita, the other bar girl, laughed and joked with them, appearing to enjoy their attention. So, Diana's tables never seemed to fill up as often as Anita's.

She would make less money in the lounge in the evening with smaller tips. She soon learned that the wage wasn't that great for waitressing. It was the gratuities that made it worthwhile.

She could just be thankful that she only served in the bar occasionally. She felt different about serving in the dining room, not just because the tips were more plentiful but because the dinner guests were more pleasant than drinkers.

One night, when she was in the lounge, Lionel showed up and sat at one of her tables. Diana didn't want to serve him. It had been quite a jolt to see him walk in. She stood there, stunned. Jack, the bartender, spoke, "there is a customer at one of your tables, Diana," snapping her out of her shock.

Anita walked up to the bar at that moment. Diana asked her to attend Lionel but didn't use his name. She just said table three.

Anita refused, saying, "my tables are all occupied. I have too many customers now.

Diana finally walked over to Lionel. "Can I help you?"

"Yes, I will have a draft beer on tap and you. Good evening, Diana."

She swung away without answering, then returned with his beer. Nervously, she plunked it on the table. He grabbed her wrist, and Diana tried to pull away.

"Sit, Diana, you aren't that busy. I need to talk to you."

"I can't sit with the customers," she said, trying to extract her hand.

"I said sit, Diana." He squeezed her wrist tighter. The pain was excruciating. Diana sat.

"Well, Diana, it is nice to see you. When did you start working here?" his voice loaded with sarcasm. He was not happy to see his wife serving in a bar.

"I don't usually work in the lounge. I mostly work in the dining room."

"If you came home, you wouldn't need to work at all. Diana, it is time for you to come home." His voice had taken on a fit of threatening anger.

"I can't, Lionel. I am never returning to you." Her hand was numb from the pressure on her wrist, which tightened even more at her answer.

She was worried that he might snap the bones in her wrist. His hold was so powerful.

Jack arrived at the table. "Diana, you are not supposed to sit with the customers. People are waiting for service." He was sizing up the situation. This man obviously knew Diana. He didn't like the way the guy was holding her wrist.

Lionel said through gritted teeth, "get lost, buddy. This woman is my wife. I need to talk to her."

Jack knew he had better leave by the pained expression on Diana's face.

"Sorry," said Jack. He did not want to alert this man of his intention to call the police. Jack casually walked back towards the bar, stopping to take orders from two other tables. Then he continued back to the bar.

Fortunately, Lionel's back was to Jack. So, he didn't see him pick up the phone to call 911. After he made the drinks for the orders he took, he delivered them to the tables.

His eyes were watching Diana's face. Her husband was still maintaining his crushing grip on her wrist. Her eyes were shining with tears that she was trying to hold back. She did not want them to escape to her cheeks.

Jack was afraid that if he interfered that he would indeed crush or break her wrist.

"Diana, you are coming home now. I will not have my wife working in a bar. Having men ogle you and touch you is not acceptable. I know what drinkers are like."

"Lionel, I am not going home with you. Let me go. You are hurting me. If I scream, you will have every man in this room on you." The tears were escaping. Her hand was completely numb and tingly, and she had excruciating pain in her wrist.

"Diana, I said you are leaving now." Lionel was so intent on Diana's acceptance that he missed the arrival of the police until they stepped up to the table.

"I think you had better release this young lady's hand now. I am not going to ask you twice," the officer said in a brisk voice. The officer was quite burly. He looked like he could back up the claim his angry voice implied.

Lionel loosened his grip. He didn't let go completely. "It is okay, officer. This is my wife." Lionel smiled as though he had the right to treat her this way.

"I said, release her hand." The officer now had a paralyzing grip on Lionel's wrist, forcing him to release Diana. She quickly dragged her hand away, cradling it against her body. The pain increased with the flow of blood.

"I said this is my wife." Lionel was trying to break the officer's grip. So, his voice came out in a pained way.

"Is that right, ma'am?"

"We are separated and have been for almost a year," Diana said in a weak voice. Not wanting this situation to escalate at her place of employment. She needed to keep her job. "I work here. He came in, so I had no choice but to serve him." Diana arose while she was talking.

Jack was at the table. He put his arm around Diana, pulling her away from the table, as he said, "come, Diana, let the police handle it now."

"I think we should be leaving now, don't you?" The officer was looking at Lionel intently. "I don't want any fuss, so come quietly." He had loosened his grip but still retained Lionel's arm to assist him up from the chair.

Lionel knew he didn't have much choice. He got to his feet, proceeding the officer from the bar followed by the other officer. They put him in the back of the patrol car, which had a screen between the back and front seat. One officer stayed to talk with him. The other officer went back in to speak to Diana. She was now sitting at the bar, holding her arm while Jack talked to her.

"Are you all right, Miss?" the officer asked.

Jack said, "her wrist is very bruised. I think she should have ice for it. I have been trying to talk her into going home."

"You can get the ice. I need to talk to her."

Jack dipped his head to the officer then moved behind the bar.

"Your name?"

"Diana Cardwell."

"That man is your estranged husband?"

"Yes, his name is Lionel Cardwell."

"Are you in divorce proceedings?"

"No, I don't have the money for a divorce. I don't even have a legal separation."

"Maybe you should think about it, Miss," the officer suggested.

Diana looked like a gentle lady to him. He hated the idea that Lionel still had legal control over her.

Diana said thoughtfully, "I think I will now. I have been saving my wages for that express purpose, but I haven't made much progress. I have just started working here."

After Jack applied the ice to her wrist, he stayed close to her to give her his support. He liked Diana. She was too gentle a person for the likes of Lionel.

Diana's mind flew to Lucinda's braces, which was her original reason for obtaining work, along with being independent of Lucy. Lucy had said she had things to set in place before Eric and she would live together as man and wife. So, Diana had put her independence on the back burner for a bit, so maybe now she could work towards getting a divorce.

The young officer noticed Diana was more deeply disturbed by the situation than he first suspected.

"Miss, are you sure you are all right? Maybe you know someone who will drive you home?" Looking towards Jack, whom he noticed, was being quite supportive.

"No, I will be all right. I need to keep busy. My customers are waiting," looking around quickly. Diana was afraid of losing her job if there was any kind of fuss made.

"Just a few more questions. How long have you been married?"

"Six years."

"How long have you been separated from him?"

"Almost a year. I had a baby. Lionel refuses to allow her to come home because she isn't perfect. She has to wear braces on her legs." The young officer and Jack were stunned. Lionel obviously had a disability the way he walked. The two men were looking at each other in amazement.

"Maybe he feels different now. Maybe that is why he wants you back," the young officer said.

"Oh, no. Lionel still only wants me back. He won't have anything to do with Lucinda. Lucinda is my baby."

"I'm sorry to hear that. Again, I would suggest you start divorce proceedings. Or at least a legal separation. Because in the eyes of the law, Lionel is still your legal husband. The police can't stop him if he is near you unless he is physically abusing you. I'm sorry, but that is the way the law works."

"I understand." Diana just wanted this to be over. She needed this job. She was afraid that if she didn't start to work, they might let her go.

The officer headed for the door.

The ice had helped with the pain in her wrist, which let her serve her waiting customers. Jack was back behind the bar but not happy about her return to work.

The customers were pleasant to her, considering how long they had been waiting for service. Most of them had witnessed Lionel's behavior toward her. They felt sorry for her, leaving a more substantial tip. The rest of the evening passed without incident. Jack waylaid her before she could leave.

"Sit, and have a drink with me."

"No, I need to get home." Diana didn't want to have to explain Lionel to anyone. It was unfortunate that he chose her place of work to harass her.

"Diana, I think you need a drink to relax you before you drive home. I don't need to know the entire situation if you don't want me to. I just need to know that you are all right. Now, please sit. What can I make for you?"

"A very weak drink. I don't like liquor much. I guess that it is an acquired taste that I have never attained."

Jack mixed her a drink with ½ shot of liquor in it. He did not want her to have after-effects since she was driving. He just wanted to talk to her to ensure that she wouldn't be alone when she went home.

Diana said regretfully, "Jack, I am truly sorry that this happened here. I need this job badly. I hope you make the others understand that. I know they will question you about what happened."

"Don't sweat it, Diana. It is not your fault your ex-husband is a jerk. Seriously, Diana, you need to consider getting a legal separation or a divorce. Divorce would be better. He still has a hold over you since you haven't done anything legal to end it."

"I know. But I have just started here, and my wage hasn't been enough for a divorce. I can't explain right now, but I have another situation that requires money also. Thank you for the drink and your concern. It did help, plus you did too. I have to get home before Lucy sends the police for me." She had gathered up her purse and jacket as she spoke.

Jack helped her put on her jacket. "Don't worry about your job. I will smooth things over for you. I want you to know that if you ever want a shoulder to lean on. I am your man."

"Thank you. I appreciate that immensely."

They said their goodnight. Diana headed out the door. When she arrived in the parking lot, which was well lit, she headed directly to Lucy's car. Lucy had insisted that she use her car if she was going to be working at night.

She looked around before she got in the car. She wondered where Lionel was? Was he still at the police station, or was he lurking around? Then she noticed Jack standing watching her from the doorway. That reassured her. She gave him a wave and got into the car.

Diana knew it was only a matter of time before Lucy would marry Eric.

Diana had been trying to build up her savings account for the possibility of having to find new accommodations. How could she use the money for a separation or divorce? Lucinda needs a home before I need a divorce or even a separation which she felt sure Lionel would not let her have without retaliation.

When she arrived home, Lucy asked her about her night. Diana replied, "I worked in the lounge bar. Not my favorite, but otherwise okay." She didn't want to alarm Lucy. She was sure Lucy would tell Troy if she let on about Lionel.

She knew Troy was pressing her not to work at night. Occasionally, Troy came in to eat dinner at the Inn. Then he would follow her home afterward, letting her know that he cared about her being out late at night. His brotherly attitude was comforting. But she wanted to be more self-sufficient when Lucy and Eric were sharing their new marital bliss.

**

Lionel had not fared well by his night's activity. When the officer put Lionel's name on the computer, it lit up with warning signs. He brought up his record of the kidnapping. Officer Rafferty quickly read the details. Indeed, this blighter did abandon his baby. It was a result of the crash during a police chase that had made Lionel a cripple.

"Larry, I think you should read this."

Larry was the officer who had interviewed Mrs. Cardwell. He came over to the computer and scanned the screen.

"That is exactly what Mrs. Cardwell said, but I didn't quite believe her. No man could do such a thing." The two officers squared their shoulders. They were going to be quite happy to interrogate Mr. Cardwell with no holds barred. The original reporting officers were at another station. They decided to give them a call first.

Officer Jackson was off duty but had stopped at the station to pick up a book from his locker. He took the call. "Well! Well! Mr. Cardwell is still up to his old tricks, is he? Well, I would like to throw the book at him. He got off too lightly on the kidnapping charge because the judge deemed that losing his leg was punishment enough. So, he got off with a reprimand."

He continued. "Any man who would walk away from that gorgeous baby deserves severe punishment. She has problems with her legs, but Dr. Sawyer said a correction was easy. You should have seen the baby. She is an absolute doll. Besides, it was probably his bad genes that caused the problem with her legs. Don't go easy on him. Put the fear of God into him. Mrs. Cardwell is a nice lady who shouldn't have married him in the first place."

Officer Rafferty thanked him. Then he passed the information on to Larry. With purposeful steps, they walked into the interrogation room where Lionel sat.

They repeatedly questioned him about his legs, making Lionel explain his affliction in detail, which Lionel did in an annoyed voice. Then they talked about his beautiful baby that Officer Jackson described. Lionel only sneered at that remark.

Then Officer Rafferty criticized Lionel for his faulty genes, which had probably caused his daughter's legs to be abnormal at birth. Lionel was adamant, never backing down where his daughter was concerned.

Lionel angrily refused to talk about Lucinda. Every time they mentioned her. He clammed up and looked at the mirror on the wall. Knowing it was a two-way mirror and that someone was probably watching and judging him.

Lionel was adamant, never backing down where his daughter was concerned.

He wanted Diana back only. He wanted the life they had before his daughter was born. The truth of the matter was, he never wanted children at all. He only said he wanted the baby because Diana got pregnant. Not by choice. Besides, what these officers were saying couldn't possibly be true. It couldn't have been my bad genes.

His voice was loud and accusing with bitterness when he said, "I always knew Diana was inferior, so it was her genes, not mine." Then he clammed up.

It had taken many months of his complaining before she finally got it right, the meals and the meticulously clean house. That was what he wanted again. Diana's undivided attention to his home. His goal was his home the way he liked it. No matter what others thought about this situation. Diana was his.

The officers were aware that Lionel was not listening to them. They couldn't book him on a charge other than domestic disturbance. So, that meant Mrs. Cardwell would have to charge him. They didn't believe that she would do that. So, they decided to detain him overnight in a cell anyway.

"Well, Lionel, it looks like we will be providing the accommodation for tonight."

"You can't do that. You have to charge me first."

"No, that isn't quite true. You have been uncooperative. We are giving you a rest until you can better answer our questions."

"I want to call my lawyer."

"Fine, you have the right. But you will still be spending the night," Officer Rafferty said with great relish.

Lionel's call to his lawyer didn't bode well. He was out of town on vacation.

Officer Rafferty liked the sound of the cell door clanging. After hearing what Lionel had done to his wife and daughter, he felt a deep satisfaction in the sound. He knew he couldn't hold Lionel any longer than overnight. Maybe Lionel would be ready to mend his thinking after his jail stay. It was such a positive message.

Rafferty thought about Mrs. Cardwell. How could such a lovely lady get tangled up with the likes of Lionel? He hoped Diana would heed the advice Larry gave her about getting a separation or divorce. Lionel didn't deserve any second chance to get his wife to come back to him, especially without the baby.

When he walked back towards the front desk, he could hear foul language and turmoil going on. The usual night activities of the station.

He met Larry coming towards him. He gave him a thumbs-up sign. "One more for the good guys."

"I've done the report. If you want to add anything, I saved it under jerk," said Larry with a grin.

Chapter Fifteen

Diana was not taking the events lightly. She couldn't sleep. What was she going to do to stop Lionel? If he caused her any more trouble at the Inn, she would lose her job. Perhaps she should take Lucinda and move away. It was apparent that Lionel had no intention of giving up. He also had made it clear that he still didn't want Lucinda, even though he had half a leg and a limp in the other. He still didn't want his imperfect daughter. She had tried to explain to him how her legs had almost straightened naturally. When she had mentioned the braces, he had changed the subject to only wanting her back as his wife.

She knew, even if he had offered to take them both back. She could never go back to him. His regimental perfection was too much. Cans by size and color in the cupboard. The cushions on the sofa just so.

Lucinda's attire would have to be spotless at all times. She wouldn't be allowed to cry or play in the living room. Her toys would not be allowed anywhere except in her bedroom and possibly Lucinda too. How could she have thought a baby would improve things for them? Maybe it was for the best that Lucinda's legs had driven them apart. Not that she wanted Lucinda to have a slight imperfection. Diana knew she could never live there ever again.

She was still no closer to sleep. Diana got up to get a hot drink, so she went to the kitchen and filled the kettle, setting it on the stove to heat. Hearing steps in the hall, Lucy appeared in the doorway. "Can't you sleep? Do you have a problem? I thought when you came home tonight that you were upset about something. You were, weren't you? Now talk. I am here to listen."

"Lionel came to the bar tonight. He grabbed me by the wrist, almost breaking it. Jack called the police. They took Lionel away. The police said I should file for separation or divorce because otherwise, I was still legally his wife, even if we aren't living together. I don't have the money as I am trying to save for when you marry and go to live with Eric, which will be soon, no doubt," Diane's voice was sad. Then she added, "of course, I am happy for you. Eric is wonderful, and you do make a wonderful couple. I don't know why you are hesitating about setting a date." The kettle had boiled. She was making chamomile tea.

Lucy said with a lilt in her voice. "Eric and I have set a date for one month from Friday. I didn't say anything yet because I was trying to decide what to do about the house. I knew you would worry. Troy and I talked about what would be best for me. We have decided that I should keep the house until market prices improve. So, I think I will be renting. I have been giving it a great deal of thought all evening. It wasn't until I went to bed that the natural person to rent would be you and Lucinda. Would you like to be my renter?"

Diana picked up her tea, taking a big sip to give herself time to think. It was happening. Should she take the opportunity, or should she move somewhere else? Maybe she should move to another town away from Lionel.

"I will charge a reasonable amount. Maybe you can get another job that pays more. As you will need a full-time babysitter for Lucinda anyway," said Lucy trying to be helpful.

"It is not that. I am debating about moving to another town to get away from Lionel."

"Oh, Diana, it must have been terrible for you. Lionel appearing and mistreating you. I'm sorry that I didn't say something sooner. It is just that I have been caught up in this housing problem all evening. It is hard to get past it."

"Lucy, I will lose my job if he does it again. They are not going to like having to call the police all the time. Then what will I do?"

"You know, compared to your problem, mine is minor. I know you think it would be best to move somewhere else. But the way Lionel is so persistent, I think he would find you wherever you went. Besides, at least here you have Troy and your friends in the park. They won't let Lionel get you."

"Yes, maybe you're right. But I won't be able to pay you enough for this place. You would get so much more if you advertised."

"Yes, but then I would be getting a stranger. Who might not take care of the house the way you will?" Lucy could not let Diana know that Troy had been paying her wage, not Lucy. Now he wanted to continue to pay part of her rent.

She had asked him why he was doing that, knowing full well what his answer would be. Troy had said he had come to love Diana and Lucinda. But he also knew Diana would not be receptive to his love until she was free from Lionel. He just needed to keep her here in high hopes of a divorce eventually.

Troy had made her swear on their grandmother's grave, whom they had both loved, that Lucy would never breathe a word of this to Diana. Lucy knew that Troy had tried to talk Diana into moving in with him. But she had refused naturally. Troy had said it would have been platonic if she had. Lucy had commented, 'wouldn't that only have been more challenging for you. Besides, Diana is not the type of person to look for charity. She is too independent.'

Diana was in a quandary. Should she stay at Lucy's house, or should she leave to go elsewhere? Lucy was right. Lionel would probably find her wherever she went.

"All right. I will look after your house for you. Lucinda likes it here, and being close to the park is a bonus. It is far nicer than I could afford elsewhere."

Lucy hugged Diana. "Thank you for seeing it my way. I need a clear mind to start preparing for my wedding, which Eric wants to be small but not too small. He wants me to wear white. I told him I couldn't do that. But he said it was his first wedding. So, he wanted it all. So, we compromised. I am wearing an ivory lace gown with white sleeves and a white veil. We picked it out together when we were in Seattle one weekend. He also gave me this," pulling out a ring on a chain from under her nightgown.

"Oh, Lucy, why aren't you wearing it? Was it because of me?" Diana held the ring in her fingers. The light made the diamond twinkle in rainbow colors.

"Yes. I knew you were worried about me leaving."

"Put it on. I want to see it on your finger. I am sorry that you couldn't share Eric's gift, feeling you had to hide it. I love you, Lucy. You are so protective of my feelings."

Lucy slipped the ring on her finger with a smile. Memories returned of when Eric knelt, and his knee cracked had made her laugh. Then he had admonished her to be serious, as he was only going to do this once. Then he had said, 'Lucy, I give you this ring along with my heart to have and to hold forever. Will you be my wife? To marry me and love me forever.' His knee creaked again. Lucy tried to keep a straight face. Then the occasion struck her. Tears filled her eyes as Eric slipped the ring on her finger, kissing the finger that had accepted his ring.

Lucy smiled through her tears. 'Yes, I will marry you. I want to love you forever,' Eric quickly rose to his feet and pulled her into his arms. The kiss started with the promise of love for the future. Then he deepened the kiss until passion consumed them. He picked her up in his arms and took her to bed so that he could love her more deeply. To let the love they shared complete their vows of love to each other.

Diana brought her back from her reverie. "Lucy, it is such a beautiful ring. There must be a lot of love attached to it. I am so happy for you both."

They hugged each other, realizing how much they were going to miss this companionship. Lucy and Diana felt like their close relationship made them almost sisters.

"You will enjoy my house. I feel better about that. I will come back to visit you whenever I can. After all, you and Lucinda are family to me. Now, should we head for bed?"

Diana glanced at the clock. It was 3:30 AM to her amazement.

"Yes, we had better call it a night. I am sorry to have kept you awake. I will take care of your house. I will always have the bedroom ready for you and Eric." Then she added with a grin, "sister." Again, a hug before heading upstairs to see if they could salvage the night for sleep.

**

The day of the wedding arrived. Lucy's parents were looking after Lucinda because Diana was the maid of honor.

Lucinda's pretty dress of frills and lace in pink satin came almost to her ankles. She wore a crown of flowers in her hair.

When Lucy's parents arrived, they walked up the aisle, each holding one of Lucinda's hands. Lucinda was walking now. Even though the braces gave her a stiff-legged gait, she was quite proficient with them.

Stopping every few steps, Mr. Sawyer placed the basket within reach for Lucinda to throw rose petals around in front of her. Her blond curls and blue eyes captivated everyone as they passed. Her few baby teeth showed in a smile, and she emitted the occasional giggle.

Eric and Troy stood at the altar, awaiting the maid of honor and bride. When Lucinda finally reached the front of the church, she spied Troy.

When Troy's parents should have directed Lucinda into their seats, she pulled away. She walked unerringly to Troy, grabbing his pant leg, putting up her face, puckering her lips for a kiss. Troy bent over to comply quickly. Then she did the same to Eric. He bent down to kiss her too. Lucinda walked over to Troy's waiting parents amid the awes from the crowd and the clapping. Troy and Eric were now wearing the biggest grins, and their nervousness was gone.

Diana and Lucy were waiting for Lucy's father to reappear to escort Lucy down the aisle. They both knew something had pleased the crowd. But because they were in the vestibule, they couldn't see what had happened. They only heard the awes and the clapping.

Lucy's Dad arrived with a big grin. "Lucinda was a hit."

"What did she do?" Diana asked anxiously.

"She did the flower bit with panache. Then she stole the show, walking by herself to Troy and Eric, insisting on a kiss from each of them."

"Oh, dear," said Diana.

"No, it was so cute. Lucinda stole everyone's heart." He turned to Lucy.

"Now, my dear daughter, it is your turn to shine." He kissed Lucy. "Did I tell you how lovely you look?"

"Yes, Dad, three times," responded the smiling Lucy.

"And you, Diana, are a picture of beauty too." Diana beamed.

Her father took Lucy's arm. "Are we ready?"

The wedding march started as Diana appeared in the doorway. She walked down the aisle in her pink satin and lace dress. She wore a crown of pink rosebuds encircled by white baby's breath in her hair and a similar bouquet in her hands.

Troy drew in a breath at Diana's beauty. He wished that she was marrying him. Troy would have been delighted if Diana was coming to him in love because he knew he loved her very much. Diana smiled at him as she reached her place at the altar.

Eric was spellbound by his bride's loveliness and her father's proud grin. The smiling guests watched their progression to the altar.

The minister asked, "who gives this bride in Holy Matrimony?"

Lucy's father replied as he placed Lucy's hand in Eric's hand. "I give you my daughter to love her as I have forever."

Eric grasped Lucy's hand, murmuring, "I accept."

"Dearly beloved, we are present here to witness the joining of Lucy Ann Gardner and Eric Lee Stewart in Holy Matrimony." Eric and Lucy were staring at each other in love. While Troy kept his gaze centered on Diana, wishing those words were for them.

The bride and groom made personal vows and exchanged wedding rings. Then the minister pronounced them husband and wife. "You may kiss the bride." Eric lifted Lucy's veil reverently. The kiss he bestowed on her was filled with love and promise. After they appeared back from signing the register, the minister presented them as Mr. and Mrs. Stewart.

The wedding couple started down the aisle with happy grins. Diana and Troy followed them.

When they reached the pew where Lucinda was with Troy's parents, Lucinda was standing, ready to join them. Troy and Diana each took one of her hands, making their way up the aisle slowly. Lucinda was smiling happily at everyone. Then she glanced up at Troy. He gave her a wink, and she looked up at her mother and giggled with happiness to the enjoyment of the wedding guests.

The photographer took pictures, capturing these special moments, as well as the kisses Lucinda had bestowed on Troy and Eric. The picture taking over, they headed to the reception at the Castleton Inn.

Troy pranced attendance on Diana and Lucinda. When the music piece slowed, he picked up Lucinda, then pulled Diana up, his arm encased her, and the three danced. Lucinda was having great fun. She kissed each of them on the cheek. Then she indicated for Diana and Troy to kiss. The kiss soon slipped from Diana's cheek to her mouth. Diana didn't want the dance to end.

The band played three slow numbers together. So, Troy enjoyed dancing through all three. Lucinda kept up the kissing game.

By the third dance, Diana's and Troy's kisses were passionately longer. Troy was taking full advantage of Lucinda's idea of kissing, no longer a game for Troy. He liked kissing Diana too much to want to stop.

Neither was aware that the music had ended until they heard clapping. Then Troy and Diana realized that they had an audience to their tender moment. They guiltily broke apart.

Diana's blush was slow to recede from her red cheeks after realizing that they had an audience. Lucinda thought this was great fun and wanted more.

But the band had switched to a faster piece, so Troy guided them off the floor. They went to sit with Troy's parents. Hoping that they had not witnessed their performance on the dance floor. Mrs. Sawyer's manner didn't show any sign that she had seen anything.

Mr. Sawyer Sr. immediately took Lucinda on his knee, bouncing her around to the music's beat.

Mrs. Sawyer told Diana how attractive she and her adorable daughter looked today.

Diana couldn't look at Troy yet, not until she got her emotions under control.

Eric and Lucy joined them, taking the limelight off of Diana. The conversation became a light bantering all around.

The next set of dances were slow ones. Mr. Sawyer Sr. asked his daughter to dance. Eric followed suit, holding out his hand to Mrs. Sawyer. But she said she wasn't dancing tonight. So, Eric picked up Lucinda whipping her onto the dance floor. Troy took the opportunity to ask Diana.

Diana answered, "no, I'll sit this out with your mother."

"No way, dear. You go and enjoy yourself. Troy, take her onto the dance floor. I will be fine," she said with a cheery smile.

Troy held out his hand. Diana placed her hand in his, both remembering their last three dances.

When they reached the dance floor, Troy pulled her close, linking his arms around her back. Diana shyly slipped her arms around Troy's neck. Their bodies melded together, barely moving, enjoying the feelings flowing between them. Diana couldn't break contact with his eyes or his body. She wanted this so much. Troy appeared to desire her. Was it possible?

The embrace was not brotherly by any means. They were mesmerized by each other. Troy was raining fairy kisses on her hair, her forehead, her temple, then her cheeks. When he finally reached her yearning lips, they fused together, swaying in place. The music and dancers tuned out in their fascination with each other.

Their kiss had gone from passion to desire, tingling their bodies and drawing them ever closer in response. Troy knew that he had to stop. But how could he? Finally, breaking apart, they both looked guiltily around. No one was paying them any attention, thankfully. Troy pulled her back into his arms.

He whispered, "Diana, I love you."

"Troy, I am not free."

"I know, but I had to tell you how I feel. I can't keep it to myself any longer."

"We shouldn't have kissed," Diana treasured his confession of love, a result of the passionate kisses they were sharing.

"Diana, I have wanted to kiss you for so long. I couldn't help myself. You are a fairy princess tonight. How could I not kiss you?" Their steps had slowed to sway again. They were so intent on each other.

"Troy, I can't accept this while I am still married." Reality had set in for Diana.

"I know. That is why I have never let you know how I feel before now."

Eric and Lucinda were dancing by. Lucinda put out her arms for Troy. "Da, Da."

Eric passed Lucinda to Troy. Then Eric claimed Diana and danced her away. She didn't want to leave Troy, but at the same time, she was glad of the interruption from the inflamed feelings running rampant through her.

"You look ravishing tonight, Diana," Eric spoke with a caressing voice, "or should the word be ravished?" his voice breaking into teasing laughter. Diana blushed, hiding her face in his shoulder.

Lucy's laughing voice said. "Hey! He is my man." After Eric passed the laughing Diana off to Mr. Sawyer's ready arms, Eric drew Lucy into his loving arms.

Diana was thankful that there was subdued lighting. Maybe, Mr. Sawyer Sr. wouldn't notice her heightened color. Or maybe, he was just too gallant to comment.

The bride and groom departed soon after Diana caught the bride's bouquet. She felt Lucy had deliberately thrown it her way, even though her back was towards the waiting hands. They waved the happy couple off on their honeymoon.

Troy was standing beside her, holding Lucinda. Diana suggested that they leave, mentioning that she had to put Lucinda to bed. Troy gave her a loving smile. Letting her know that he knew she was avoiding dancing with him again. However, he did think it was for the best. They went to find his parents to say goodnight.

When they reached home, Diana was quite distant. Troy knew the magic was over. Lucinda had fallen asleep on the ride home. Troy carried her inside to her bed.

Troy touched Diana's cheek with a caressing finger. Then he quickly left before she could express herself and defame the evening's passionate events.

The magic of the night melted into a memory.

Chapter Sixteen

At first, it was strange for Diana to have the house to herself. She kept waiting, expecting Lucy to appear only to remember Lucy was married. Even Lucinda kept asking for Lucy. Diana was having trouble explaining that Lucy wouldn't be around much anymore to someone so young.

Diana found it difficult at first because her days while living with Lucy had been structured around Lucy's routine, whether work or pleasure time. Now that was gone. Her days seemed to be without direction.

Diana had a new babysitter, Kathy, a teenager from down the street. Lucinda took to Kathy right away. She was the scholarly type, always delving into books, either for school or a thirst for knowledge. She regularly arrived weighed down with an enormous book bag.

Kathy loved children. She asked Diana to refrain from bathing Lucinda and getting her ready for bed before she left. Kathy enjoyed the bath time as part of her playtime with Lucinda. She was careful to replace the braces on Lucinda until bedtime after her bath.

Diana was going to work earlier to get more hours, so she provided dinner for Kathy and Lucinda each day. Diana was amazed at how well Lucinda related to Kathy so quickly. Her excitement each day for Kathy to appear always started about an hour ahead of time.

Diana and Lucinda were still going to the park almost daily except when it rained, of course. She was always careful to never let Lucinda out of her sight. She had not heard or seen Lionel since that fateful night when the police had taken him away from the Inn.

Troy was an absentee person, also. Since Lucy's wedding, he seemed to be elusive with Lucy not residing here anymore. However, Troy did telephone quite often, but he never came to the house.

This hurt Diana. She wondered if the reason was the passionate kisses at Lucy's wedding they shared? She had denied him further kisses due to her marriage. No kisses, no Troy was what his absence meant evidently. Maybe, he didn't care after all.

Poor Lucinda, Diana could see she was missing him a lot. She remembered the moment of pleasure Troy experienced when Lucinda called him 'dada.' Lucinda would often say 'dada,' letting Diana know she was missing him.

One day she was at the park with her friends and their children. Troy put in an appearance. She wasn't aware of his approach until she heard the excitement in Lucinda's voice as she called out, "dada." Her arms outstretched to his advancing muscular body. Diana whipped around to see Troy was almost upon her.

"Troy, where did you come from?" Troy lifted Lucinda into his arms as he greeted Diana.

"From your place. When I found you were gone, I headed here with high hopes." Lucinda was still saying "dada" in between smacking kisses on his cheek. Troy laughed at Lucinda's exuberance. Then she stopped, pointing at her mother, "kish."

"That is a good idea." He leaned over to place a kiss on Diana's mouth. It started as a brief touch, but somehow it evolved into more.

Diana was so intent on her daughter's reaction to Troy when Lucinda directed him to kiss her, Diana automatically let him. But then her lips betrayed her and returned the kiss willingly. Something she couldn't imagine she would ever do. Their eyes were locked together as Diana's face showed a red tinge of embarrassment.

Her friends were saying, "don't we get an introduction to the hunk? Imagine Lucinda's first words, 'dada and kish' who taught her that?"

"This is Audrey Blanchard and Betty Crosby. The hunk, as you called him is Dr. Sawyer."

Troy cut in, "Troy to you ladies," shaking hands with both of them.

"A doctor, no less. My doctors were never like you," said Audrey with a leer.

Troy answered with a lilt in his voice, "well, there are few of us around." His grin made him even more delectable.

Cowan and Nancy pushed their way into the circle. Audrey said, "this is my son Cowan. That is Nancy, who belongs to Betty. Well, I think we should be going. We have been here long enough," grabbing Cowan's hand.

"Yeah." Betty quickly put Nancy in her stroller. "We should be going too." Then called, "Nathan, we are going home."

"Was that obvious, or what?" Diana said as the two mothers made a quick exit.

"Yeah, a guy could get a complex," Troy said lightly, not wanting to allude to the fact that the disappearing ladies had quickly bowed out as a result of the kiss. They probably think there could be more without them around.

"Let's head for home." He put Lucinda in the stroller. He was tickling her to hear her happy giggles. Her sparkling eyes were gazing up at him with the pleasure of his being here at last. Diana patiently waited while thinking about the naturalness of his kiss. But she shouldn't be reading too much into the kiss. There was still Lionel in her life.

When they got home, Diana asked him to stay for lunch, and he complied gladly. Her mind quickly ran to the fridge and cupboards for a meal that could be easy and quick. Then she remembered the casserole that she had frozen for this type of occasion. It would only take approximately 40 minutes. Hopefully, he intended to stay longer than that. No maybe, she should make an omelet with cheese and mushrooms. Yes, that would be easy and less time.

"Hello in there. Did I lose you?" Troy was trying to get her attention.

But she was viewing the food options in her mind. "Just mentally looking around the kitchen for a quick lunch."

"Well, if it's going to be a problem, we could always go out to eat."

"No, I managed to sort out a feasible lunch for us. I would rather not go out."

"Okay, Diana, if you are sure. I don't want to put you out. I just wanted to spend some time with you and Lucinda."

Diana made the omelets while Lucinda and Troy played with blocks, which he promptly removed from the table when the meal was ready. Diana placed Lucinda's dish on her high-chair tray. Lucinda mostly ate with her fingers. She liked her omelet. Lucinda hadn't mastered her tiny fork or spoon, which had been a gift from Lucy. She tipped her spoon too much, causing the food to fall off, so she reverted to her hands.

Diana proudly carried the omelets to the table. They were a fluffy, cheesy perfection laced with mushrooms and red peppers. Troy complimented her on the delicious lunch.

After finishing their lunch, Troy and Diana sat in the living room. Troy was sitting on the sofa while Lucinda piled her menagerie of animals around him. He was pleased to see how Lucinda was walking quite effortlessly, despite the braces. Maybe that was because Lucinda had been wearing them for short periods before she walked. Therefore, she was more receptive as she had never walked without them.

Diana talked about work. She said how much she was enjoying it now that she was in the dining room full time. She acknowledged that working in the lounge bar wasn't something she relished. She didn't have to fear Lionel would show up again, thank goodness. As he seldom liked to eat out, she was safe in the dining room.

Troy mentioned some incidents that had happened to him since he had last seen her. When he ran out of things to say, he slipped in. "Diana, have you thought any more about getting a divorce?"

"Yes, but I can't approach any lawyer until I have more money saved."

Lionel had appeared once at the playground, but he hadn't approached her. The deterrent was her friends, Betty and Audrey. He just stood watching them from a distance.

"Will you let me help you with the funds? You could pay me back later. I think that it would be wise if you got a divorce, as the police officer suggested." He included the police recommendation in high hopes.

Troy, didn't want to let on at this time that he had a vested interest in her getting her divorce. However, he also knew that Diana would hesitate about taking his money. She had expressed on several occasions that there was no way that she would take anything from him. She felt the divorce was her duty to obtain.

In a way, he wished Lucy hadn't provided the house for Diana's use. Then maybe he would have had more success in installing her in his home. As that thought wandered through his mind, he knew it was only hopeful fiction. There was no way Diana would live with him as long as she was still married. He knew that he wanted Diana and Lucinda to be a genuine part of his life, not a platonic situation.

"No, Troy, I have to do this myself. You have done more than enough already. We can still be friends. But if I owe you money, it will probably change our relationship. I don't want that to happen. Can you understand that?"

"Yes, but I also understand that as long as you are still married to Lionel, he will keep trying to get you back. At what cost? That is my worry. I want to protect you and Lucinda. But our hands are tied as long as you are still married to him. The word 'our' refers to the police as well as me."

"Troy, I want to get away from Lionel's clutches far more than you can ever imagine. But I also feel that I have to do it myself. So, it will take a little longer. But that is how I feel. Can you accept that?"

"I guess I will have to, won't I?"

The conversation changed to a lighter note. Troy brought Diana up on the latest news of Lucy and Eric and the knowledge they have settled in Los Angeles. Troy was not happy at the lengthy distance.

"Diana, mom and dad want to get together for a barbecue on the weekend. Do you have to work this weekend?"

"No, this is my free weekend. I work three weekends and get one-off. It was perfect timing on the part of your parents. You know, Troy, I am always amazed at how your parents treat Lucinda and me like family, although we are not. I like that. I miss my parents to a certain degree, but they are still siding with Lionel. So, I don't see them much."

"So, I can tell my parents you will be there?"

"Yes, I would love to go. I know Lucinda wants to for sure. They both make such a fuss over her."

"Good. I had better get going. Sorry to eat and run, but I am due back at the office shortly." He leaned over to plant a kiss on Lucinda's upturned face. Then he planted a kiss on Diana's lips before she could step away from him. "You know, I could get used to this if you would let me?" Troy walked out, leaving that message hanging in the air.

Diana reached up with her fingers and touched her lips. Yes, she could happily get used to this too. Diana had wanted to return his kiss, but he had broken away before she was able to. Lucinda's hammering on the floor broke the dreamy thought of a shared kiss.

Diana mobilized herself to Lucinda's needing a nap. She didn't close the door entirely against her dreams. Instead, she just wrapped them around her, cocooning herself with the warm thoughts.

**

At last, the day came when she filed for divorce. Troy's parents had recommended a lawyer for her when they had gone to the barbecue.

It had been a wonderful dinner. The casual flow of conversation and laughter, a bonus so that Diana left her fears behind.

After dinner, they discussed several personal matters regarding a merger Troy's dad was in the middle of achieving. Upon hearing a lawyer mentioned as a significant player in the deal prompted Diana to ask for a lawyer's name to handle her divorce.

"Does that mean you finally have the money for your divorce?" asked Troy with a gleeful smile.

"I don't know. It all depends on how much the lawyer charges. I hope so," replied Diana shyly. She didn't feel comfortable talking about this in front of Troy's parents. She had been thinking about it while Troy and his father were discussing the merger. It had just popped out.

Immediately Troy's father put forth a name, saying he was inexpensive but very skillful.

As it was getting late shortly after, they left for home.

Troy went with her to the first interview. His input had been helpful because Diana had been too nervous and embarrassed to give intimate details to a stranger. The main issue was Diana wanting to divorce Lionel for his unwarranted behavior. Troy gave the minimum information of Lionel's behavior since Lucinda's birth and his denial of his daughter as partly the reason for the divorce.

Now that Diana was more confident. The lawyer was very proficient at cutting through the details to the facts that he required. Diana was putting forward the necessary information.

Troy had only come to break the ice until Diana was ready to open up to the lawyer herself. Troy felt that the required information should be between Diana and her lawyer and excused himself. Troy amused Lucinda in the waiting room.

When she appeared back in the waiting room, Diana met Troy's gaze and gave a confident smile. Mr. Anderson was behind her.

"Lucinda, can you walk over to me? Mr. Anderson wants to meet you. I have talked so much about you." Lucinda had been standing in front of Troy, holding onto his knee. She had turned towards her mother in reaction to the door opening. Lucinda quickly stepped away from Troy to head for her mother with a big smile. Lucinda liked to walk even though the braces were hampering her to a degree.

Mr. Anderson watched the little angel with her spunky blonde curls and blue eyes. Her smile of achievement lit up her face in cherub-like splendor as she moved towards them.

Diana took her hand. "Lucinda, that was wonderful. Mr. Anderson wanted to see how well you walk now. You are getting so good at it." She bent over to kiss Lucinda's cheek. Lucinda giggled with delight.

Mr. Anderson said, "Lucinda, you are very good at eating up the floor. You have a right to be proud of yourself."

Lucinda pointed to the floor. "Eat?"

"Well, maybe eating wasn't quite the word that I should've used with someone so young." He gave a small chuckle. It had been a long time since he had spoken to someone her age. His own family's youngest was now in their teens.

Gazing at Lucinda, he thought, what kind of a man could walk away from this beautiful child? He felt he was going to take great pleasure in dealing with the father's lawyer. He intended to work diligently to separate the adamant Lionel from Diana.

He recognized that Troy had a personal interest in Diana and her daughter. He had ascertained that there was love on the part of Troy, but he didn't get the impression that it was reciprocated by Diana, not openly anyway. Maybe Troy was just hopeful that he could draw her into his life after finalizing the divorce.

They said their goodbyes before Mr. Anderson invited his next client into his office.

Chapter Seventeen

Diana pushed Lucinda on the swing. They were early. Surely Audrey and Betty would be arriving soon. There was another mother with two little boys playing on the monkey bars across the playground. The boys' laughter drew her attention as they scrambled like monkeys up to the top. They shinnied down the other side with their arms and legs, scurrying in their race to outdo each other.

Lucinda's frantic jabbering drew her attention away, only to have her whole body freeze in dread as she heard.

"Diana, I will stop the divorce. You are mine. You will always be mine." Lionel's voice wasn't threatening. He was so confident in his statement that it was unnecessary to use an aggressive tone.

Diana whipped around. Lionel was standing behind her, about two feet away.

"Lionel?" The fear inside her had suppressed her voice to a whisper.

"Diana, why are you filing for divorce? You must realize that I will never consent?"

Diana grabbed Lucinda out of the swing, trying to give herself time to formulate an answer. She held Lucinda tightly in her arms, wanting to protect Lucinda and herself from Lionel's presence.

"Lionel, I want this divorce. I can never live with you again." Her voice came out sounding weak when she most wanted it to be strong and positive. She was angry at herself, which stiffened her resolve. "Lionel, this divorce will go through. Mr. Anderson said you could not possibly block it." Her voice came out more firmly.

"Diana, there is no question. I will block it. I am very confident that I will win as your lawyer is not right in his predictions. In fact, I am so confident that I will take you back now. You are mine. You will remain mine."

It was at this point that Diana recognized that Lionel was in a state of almost madness. He was decisive in his speech, but his eyes were practically trance-like. Was Lionel on drugs? Was he drunk, or had he gone mad? All Diana knew was that she was petrified for Lucinda and herself.

"Lionel, you don't seem to be well. You aren't thinking clearly. Please leave us alone." She looked frantically over at the other mother with the boys. But they were leaving the park, walking in the opposite direction. The mother was watching the playful antics of the two boys. Should she scream? Diana didn't want to involve others. They might get hurt. She would just have to keep talking, hoping that Audrey and Betty would arrive. They should be here soon.

"There is nothing wrong with me. I cannot leave you alone. You are mine. You are my wife. You will come home with me now."

Before Diana could back away, Lionel's arm extended to grasp her in a steel-like hold, which Diana couldn't shake off. She shifted Lucinda to her other arm, turning her body away as much as possible within his bruising grasp.

Lucinda started to cry, sensing her mother's fear.

"Put the child down, Diana." The steel grip tightened, motivated by his angry words. Diana cried out in pain as she let Lucinda slide to the ground. She reached for his hand to loosen it.

Lucinda wrapped herself around Diana's leg, holding onto her tightly while crying louder.

"Diana, we are leaving now. Push the child away, or I will injure her." His voice changed and was now very threatening. His hands held her upper arms against her body.

"You wouldn't hurt your daughter? How could you even consider such a thing to injure your child? A man like you doesn't deserve to have a wife."

"Yes, I would injure her because this is not my child. Look at her braces. I would never have an imperfect child." There was such conviction in his voice that struck more terror in Diana. This man was indeed in the throes of deep madness.

"Lucinda, let go of Mommy's leg. Please, darling. Mommy needs to move." She was trying to talk lovingly to Lucinda. She had to protect her child. Lucinda was so deep into fear and crying that she disobeyed her mother.

"Release yourself from that child, Diana, if you want to protect her," yelling in anger, shaking Diana in his rage. Lucinda cried louder. The way Lionel was holding onto Diana made it impossible to reach down to escape her daughter's grip.

"Lucinda, Mommy wants you to let go. I need to move. Please, darling, let go." Her voice wasn't quite so loving this time. Her fear was mounting despite her attempt to reassure Lucinda.

Lionel reached down to grab Lucinda, extracting her from her mother's leg to Lucinda's surprise. He threw her aside into a mud puddle from last night's rain. Lucinda fell in a crumpled heap, arms and legs askew, increasing her crying. Diana tried to react, but Lionel's steel-like grip was quickly joined by his free hand. He clamped on her, squeezing the circulation from her arms. He was dragging her away from the swings and the sandy area of the park.

"Lionel, you can't leave her alone. She is just a baby." Diana's face was a mass of tears and pleading. She tried to twist her body away, but his tight grip on her made it impossible to escape. Her fear mounted for her daughter. "Lionel, let me take her with me. I will do anything you say. You can't leave her here alone." Diana was frantically looking back at Lucinda, crawling after them, hampered by her braces and her tears.

Diana was trying to kick out at Lionel without success. Then she tried digging in her heels, but Lionel just lifted her clear off the ground and continued out of the park.

She was screaming, but there was no one around that she could see. Even the street was bare, where she could now see Lionel's van, a road that generally had a steady stream of traffic.

When they reached the van, Diana thought she would be able to break his hold while he fumbled with the keys. She quit struggling in readiness, but she was fooled. Lionel hadn't locked the van, and Diana's stillness aided him in hustling her inside.

Diana gave one last look back at Lucinda. No longer crawling, her pathetic body crumbled into the ground, rocking with sobs. Diana screamed and screamed until Lionel hit her, knocking her into a daze. He quickly covered her mouth with wide tape.

Lionel started the van, pulling away with a screech of tires. It was then that Diana saw Audrey and Betty approaching with their children in their strollers. Diana was relieved as the van shot by them. She knew they would go to Lucinda's aid.

The racing van caught the two women's attention because of the erratic driving. They knew that this was Lionel's van. It had been around on several other occasions. The tinted glass stopped them from seeing Diana's fearful face staring out at them. They turned away from their path to the park as though to follow the van. Diana's heart raced. *Please, don't turn away. Lucinda needs you.*

That was the last of her sight of her friends as Lionel careened around the corner, blocking her vision behind buildings. Diana's mind churned in fear for her baby. Now that her friends turned away, how soon would someone find Lucinda? Would she crawl into traffic? Would she disappear when someone found her, never to return? *Please, God, make my friends turn back for Lucinda's sake.*

Diana's heart was thumping in fear and dread. Would she be able to escape Lionel to go back for her baby? Why did she go to the park so early? She knew Audrey and Betty wouldn't be there that soon.

Why hadn't she kept a watchful eye for Lionel's van? Why didn't she notice the vehicle as it appeared on the street? Diana knew her back was to the road, but she should have been looking over her shoulder.

If only she hadn't enjoyed seeing the two boys' antics on the monkey bars, she might have seen Lionel sooner.

Diana was trying to get a hold of the door handle. If Lionel stopped for a traffic light, she could jump from the van. Diana also wanted to be ready to wave if someone was close enough to see her. But then she remembered that she could easily see out with the tinted glass, but no one could see into the vehicle. So, that plan was out, dousing Diana's spirit.

Lionel's driving had settled down to normal speed. However, Diana's mind was with her lost baby and not on Lionel's words to her.

"Diana, why are you doing this to me? I was a good husband. I provided for you. You never had to work. It was that child that did it. That child of the devil. I knew I couldn't impregnate you with an imperfect child. Diana, you will see, we will have a perfect life again. You will soon forget that devil child. Diana, you are mine. You'll see, we will have a perfect life once again."

Lionel was rubbing his knee, where his artificial limb was attached. He had twisted his body, causing his stump to swivel in the socket of his prosthesis, making it painful. Thankfully, it wasn't the leg he needed to drive the car, or it would be unbearable. He mentally thought he would inflict pain on Diana when he got her home for causing deep pain in his left leg.

Lionel picked up speed as the pain aggravated his nerves, needing his much-used painkillers. The doctor had warned him against using them continually. But the agony was seldom kept at bay. Lionel knew that taking them caused his mind to go wild. His thoughts would go askew, but he had no choice. He needed the pain wiped out.

It started to rain. Lionel engaged the window wipers. The swish-swish of the window wipers was annoying to his mind. The increased speed made his tires slide on the now slippery streets. As he turned the corner, he sent a spray of water over a pedestrian standing near a puddle. The pedestrian could be seen shaking his fist in the rearview mirror. Lionel hoped he hadn't taken his license plate number to report him.

The rain had a different effect on Diana. Her poor baby was alone in the rain-soaked park, and no one to find her. The rain would keep people away from the park. In particular, the swings and slide area would quickly turn to muddy soil from the deluge of rain that was well beyond a shower. Her tears were flowing profusely. Lionel gave her head a whack with his ringed fist.

"Stop that sniveling you don't need to cry for the Devil's child."

Diana tried to stem the flow. She wanted to keep her wits for a possible escape.

Thunder and lightning could be seen and heard in the distance. Swish-swish was the intruding noise of the wipers. With the heavy deluge, Lionel increased the wiper speed. Now, it was swish, clack, swish, clack. As with the added speed, the wiper seemed to hit the edge of the window, causing the clacking sound. Lionel hated the noisy wipers going back and forth, disrupting his vision. If Diana had cooperated, they would've been home by now.

Diana hated the wipers because that added to the horror of her daughter sobbing in the mud in the pelting rain. She was silently screaming behind the tape, which she had tried to remove. But Lionel had hit her so hard on the side of her head that she was almost unconscious.

She tried to clear her head to prepare for leaping from the car at the first opportunity, which came into place at the next intersection they were approaching. The light was changing from orange to red. Diana flexed her fingers on the door handle as the car slowed to a halt, turning herself for the leap. Push, nothing happened. Again, her hand galvanized quickly, pushing the handle down, but to no avail. The door would not open. There was no response to the moving handle. Then she realized that Lionel locked the doors so that his side of the van controlled them.

"Yes, my dear. Thanks to modern technology, the locks can be regulated by me. So, give up before you hurt yourself. You are mine, and you will remain mine forever."

Diana was trying to raise the lock button. But it would not respond. Then she noticed there were words of lock and unlock above it with a button below on the door's armrest. But again, it would not respond either way she pushed.

"Give up. I told you that I control all the locks from the driver's side. A safety feature to protect children that might be sitting in the front seat and accidentally push the button in error." He grinned openly at her futile escape attempt.

Lionel's eyes pulled back to address the bunched traffic. Diana pulled the tape from her mouth before he could backhand her. She started to scream.

Lionel's hand flew out with a fist that hit her jaw, driving her into the window, which sustained a crack from Diana's chrome barrette as it violently hit against the glass. It was a tiny crack, hardly noticeable. But the barrette had bent, driving it into the side of her head, drawing blood and causing pain. Her face was bleeding too, where his ring had dug into her tender skin.

"You are my wife. I care about you. Why do you insist on making me hit you? I don't want to injure you. Now sit back. We will be home soon."

"Lionel, you are a beast. I will never live with you or care for you anymore. You have to let me go. Lucinda's all alone in the rain." A smash of thunder followed by lightning, then more thunder intensifying the fright she was feeling.

"Lucinda will be so afraid. She doesn't like thunderstorms. Do you have no feelings at all for other human beings in distress? If you won't acknowledge her as your daughter, please, Lionel, go back and get her for my sake. I'll do anything you want if you do. I'll stop the divorce. I will come back to live with you. Please, Lionel, don't destroy your daughter, your own flesh and blood."

Diana noticed that they were in the vicinity of their old house. Lionel was indeed taking her home. How could she ever enter that house? She hated everything about it. The memories were not happy ones.

"You be quiet. Someone will pick up your daughter. They can have her. You will be mine alone. You will never get pregnant again. I had an operation to make sure of that."

Diana listened in horror. She didn't want sex with him ever again. Let alone get pregnant. Surely, Lionel couldn't be under the illusion that their marriage would ever be normal.

It was at this point that the house came into view. Her eyes flew to the house. Then to the street. There was a police car at the curb. A police officer was approaching the road from the stairs of the house. Lionel increased the pressure on the gas, speeding up to sail past the cruiser that held another cop on the radio. The car door was open. The officer was half in half out of the car talking. As the black van sped by, the officer looked up with some concern. The half-open door was torn away from him by the wind from the speeding van.

The police call that brought them there had reported a vehicle was fleeing a playground, leaving a baby abandoned and the mother missing.

Although the officer couldn't see the van's occupants, he knew that the black van belonged to the suspect by the description. The woman, he surmised, must be inside the way it sped by him.

**

The black van erratically raced by Audrey and Betty. They stopped to turn around to view the fleeing vehicle.

"Do you think that was Lionel?" Betty inquired.

"It certainly looked like it." Audrey turned back to the playground to see if Diana was there. "I don't see Diana. I wonder why he was driving so erratically?"

The two women hesitated. Should they report the speeding van? Maybe their suspicions were for no reason? "What do you think, Betty?"

"I don't know what it means."

"Do we phone the police and report it, or do we go on to the playground as if we saw nothing?"

The two women stood, considering what they should do. "I wish I knew that doctor's phone number. I want to tell him that Lionel has been here. Maybe we should phone Diana, but we won't let on about Lionel. The two women walked away from the park.

"Mama, Lucinda." Nathan was pointing. Sure, enough there was mud-splattered Lucinda crying, walking unsteadily towards the road.

"Watch Cowan," ordered Audrey as she left her stroller to run towards the crying baby, calling "Lucinda, Lucinda."

Lucinda changed direction, heading towards the voice calling her. Audrey quickly covered the ground, her fear for Diana driving her as she saw that Lucinda was alone. She whipped Lucinda up into her protective arms. "It's alright, baby. We will find your mommy."

Lucinda between draining sobs pointed at the road. "Mama, Mama." Lucinda was now hiccupping in her distress, clinging to Audrey. Audrey headed back to Betty and the children.

"That had to be Lionel. He has taken Diana. We have to call the police." They headed across the street to the houses perched there.

"This one has a car, so they must be home," said Audrey.

"Audrey, you keep the children. I'll go and call the police." Betty headed up the walkway to the house. She rang the bell, pushing it twice to make sure she aroused someone.

The front door was pulled open by an angry man. He obviously didn't like the interruption to whatever he had been doing.

Betty started talking before he could comment on his being disturbed.

"I need to borrow your phone to call the police. A woman has been kidnapped from the park across the road."

As angry as the man was at being interrupted from his painting. He could see the agitation of the woman before him. "Come in. The phone is here in the hallway." Stepping back, the man indicated the phone with his outstretched hand.

Betty dialed 911. She was moving from foot to foot as she gave the message of doom, the kidnapping of Diana Cardwell.

"How do you know that?" asked the voice.

"Because he kidnapped her once before. We saw the van speeding away. He left their child a baby abandoned in the playground."

"Who is this man?"

"Lionel Cardwell. Mrs. Cardwell's husband, but they are separated."

"You said she was kidnapped before?"

"Yes, he kidnapped her from the hospital last time."

The information fed into the computer sent up red signals. Instantly a profile on Lionel appeared on the screen and his address.

The 911 voice asked for directions to Betty's location.

A police cruiser responded to dispatch's 911 call, indicating the playground's location and the house location of Betty's call.

Betty made a call to Dr. Sawyer, knowing that he worked at Anthony General Hospital. They paged him, and he responded.

"This is Betty. We met at the park one day. I have some bad news. Lionel has kidnapped Diana. He left Lucinda behind. We have her." She repeated the address of the house as the owner said it.

"I'll be right there. Have you called the police?"

"Yes, they are coming here."

"Well, don't let them take Lucinda. Tell them I am on my way. Thanks for calling. I will be right there."

He threw down the phone and leaped towards the hospital's entrance, running at full speed dodging anyone in his path.

Chapter Eighteen

Fortunately, Troy's car was parked next to the entrance, in short-term parking. He wasn't supposed to be at the hospital because he wasn't on duty. He had only dropped in for a few minutes to check on a patient. Now, Troy was glad that he had decided to come and see little Jimmy Benton on a whim.

Troy turned the car, driving at a fast speed to the road. The traffic was heavy. He seethed that it was holding him up. At the first opportunity, he hit the roadway and shot in the direction of Lucy's house.

His first instinct was to drive to Lionel's, but that might be a wild goose chase. However, knowing Lucinda's location, he had to get to her first. She must be distressed.

"Lionel, if you harm Diana, I will personally take you out." Troy vented his ire out loud. He was speedily heading for the park and the playground area. Thank heavens, he had gone with Diana, so he knew its location.

When he arrived at the address, it was just starting to rain. He could see Audrey and Betty talking to the police on the veranda across from the playground. Audrey was holding the crying Lucinda, trying to console her.

Troy pulled in behind the police car, leaping from the vehicle. "Lucinda," Troy called.

Lucinda looked his way. "Dada! Dada!" stretching her arms out to him.

Leaping to the veranda, Troy simply removed Lucinda from Audrey's giving arms. "It is alright, baby. I have you now. We will find your mommy."

One of the officers turned to him. "Are you the baby's father?"

"No, just a close friend of the family. Lucinda has always referred to me as Dada," said Troy in explanation while hugging Lucinda tightly in his arms. Her crying subsided at last. Her head burrowed deeply into his shoulder. Her body was still heaving with the aftermath of uncontrollable crying. Then she lay drained. Her eyes closed, and she promptly went to sleep.

The police went back to questioning the women. They were relating what they had physically seen when they arrived. They told the story that Diana had shared with them about her marriage to Lionel since Lucinda's birth.

After they ran out of things to relate, the police officer turned to Troy.

"Your name?"

"Dr. Troy Sawyer."

"How did you come to be here?"

"One of the ladies called me that knew I was a close friend of Mrs. Cardwell. I believe it was you, Betty?"

"Yes, I called him. I thought he should know about Diana as he is such a close friend of hers. We were having trouble pacifying Lucinda. I felt he could be of assistance. As you can see, Lucinda trusts him completely."

Although still tear-streaked and muddy, the police saw Lucinda's now peaceful face.

"What can you add to this, Dr. Sawyer?"

"Lionel has been following Mrs. Cardwell on several occasions. He attacked her at her place of work at the Castleton Inn. I have cautioned her always to try to be with someone if she is away from the house. She usually meets up with these two ladies. I don't know why she was alone today, but it seems that Lionel took advantage of the situation."

Audrey put in, "I already explained before you arrived. We were late today because I received a phone call from my mother, wanting to know if everyone was well. She loves to talk, so it wasn't easy to get away from her. Although I didn't time it, I am sure the call ran well over half an hour into the period, which Diana would have been alone. Sorry."

"Don't be sorry. It wasn't your fault. It was bound to happen regardless of what we could do to protect Diana. Lionel is just too persistent. He must be doubly angry at her. She has started divorce proceedings." Troy finished.

"That changes things. Mrs. Cardwell has filed for divorce, you said."

"Yes, she has. I was with her when she spoke to the lawyer that is handling the divorce."

"Well, that upgrades this from domestic disturbance to official kidnapping." He went back to the patrol car to report in.

The officer returned after talking to the dispatch.

"Officer, do you know if they have made contact with the ex-husband?" Troy was concerned that the police weren't taking Diana's disappearance seriously enough.

"They have seen them, but he got away. There are police in pursuit as we speak."

"Can I take Lucinda home? Will you contact me there if you hear anything? The number in as 555 1168."

"Yes, Dr. Sawyer, you can take her home. I've written down your number. I will call you as soon as we know anything. Mr. Cardwell went home, but a police car was in front of his house, warning him. Those officers were aware that Mrs. Cardwell was missing."

The officer decided to fill Troy in on what he had learned. "The police have the license number of Mr. Cardwell's van. It shouldn't take too long. The officer that saw them couldn't see inside the van because of the tinted glass. But they assumed Mrs. Cardwell is still with him. They will get him never fear." He ended on a positive note.

Troy thanked the officers. Lucinda was so exhausted that she didn't even awaken when he placed her in the car and did up her seat belt. He hoped she would be okay as he didn't have a baby car seat for her.

Even though Lucinda was deeply asleep, she still let out an intermittent sob every once in a while, as though she had cried so hard her subconscious was still crying.

He was patting her saying reassuringly. "Mommy will be home soon, baby. The police will find them. It's going to be okay." At least, he kept telling himself that.

When Troy got to Lucy's place, fortunately, he still had a key. He let them in, intending to put Lucinda in her bed. But Lucinda had a different idea. As soon as he started undressing her, taking off the shoes and socks, she woke up. Then she started calling. "Mama?"

"Sorry, honey, mama isn't here yet. But she will be." Now Lucinda was fully awake. The memory must have come back of her mother leaving her. She started wailing and shrieking, "Mama! Mama!" Troy tried to pat her to calm her down, but she kept knocking his hands away.

"Mama! Mama!" the tears were pouring down her face.

Troy picked her up. Lucinda struggled away from him. But he drew her tightly into his body. "Dada's here for you."

Troy rocked her. Lucinda was still wildly crying and thrashing about, not ready to be calmed that easily. Troy cursed Lionel for stealing Diana.

Troy was pacing up and down, crooning to Lucinda, wanting her to stop crying. Just listening to her racking sobs was killing him. He felt so helpless. Lucinda must have sensed this.

"Dada?" Lucinda said questioningly through her sobs.

"Yes, baby, Dada has you. Dada loves you. Mama will be home soon." Lucinda's sobs were abating. She was settling down at last. Troy was thankful.

"Dada has you, baby. He will protect you. Dada loves you. Dada loves your mommy too. I intend to marry her as soon as the divorce is final. Then we will be a family. I love you, Lucinda." Troy kissed her cheek, first one, then the other.

Lucinda accepted this, her tears dried up, and she laid her head on his shoulder. Her thumb popped into her mouth. This was new to Troy, something he had never seen her do before. He wasn't about to stop her under the circumstances. Thank heavens, he had washed her muddy hands.

Troy kept pacing until he thought she was asleep. He gently lowered her into her crib. But as soon as he released her, she opened her eyes, putting up her wee arms then starting to cry, "Dada" amongst her new tears.

Troy picked her up. He knew she was feeling insecure because of being abandoned in the playground, and he expected that.

He walked downstairs to the kitchen to give her a drink. Then Troy went into the living room. He settled in the big comfortable chair, lying Lucinda against his chest. She popped her thumb into her mouth. Troy sat, patting her back until she fell asleep.

He sat thinking about Diana. Was she okay? Did Lionel hurt her? Did the police locate them? How soon would she be home?

"I would love to get my hands on you, Lionel. I would wring your neck. Just look at what you have done to your baby. When the police catch you, I will insist on testifying. So, the judge will make you pay for your behavior. No way should you get off easy this time, for what you have done to this child, even if you lose both arms and your other leg." He was so upset with Lucinda's father.

Troy watched Lucinda sleep. But he could tell that she wasn't sleeping deeply in the way carefree babies do. She was crying in her sleep like she was reliving her mother's abduction. The memory of her abandonment by her mother, at Lionel's insistence.

Should he wake her? Troy's fist closed tightly, wishing he could use it on Lionel. This was a new feeling for him as he was usually a very peaceful man.

The phone rang. Troy eased Lucinda onto the couch, covering her with the wool blanket from the back of the sofa. He hoped the caller would hold on until he got there.

"Hello."

"Dr. Sawyer?"

"Yes."

"Dr. Sawyer, this is Officer Jackson. I didn't know if I would find you there. I was on Mrs. Cardwell's case during her last kidnapping from the hospital."

"Yes, I remember you. What have you found out?"

"Nothing yet. I just wanted to inquire how the baby is? I heard Lionel left her alone in the park."

"Yes. Lucinda is asleep, but it isn't a deep sleep. I feel she is reliving her abandonment subconsciously. How could a man do that to his flesh and blood?" Troy was furious.

"I agree. The baby was so beautiful, as I recall. Why would a father not want her?"

"He has to be slightly mental. Are you assigned to the case?" Troy asked.

"No, just a personal interest when I saw the report. It mentioned you had taken the baby to her home and the phone number," replied Officer Jackson.

"Yes, I thought that was best. Do you know anything about the whereabouts of Lionel and Diana or what is happening now?"

"The car that reported in said that Lionel saw them and kept going. It was hard to tell if Mrs. Cardwell is okay because of the tinted glass windows."

"Let me know if you find out anything. I will keep the baby in the meantime."

"Yes, I will let you know as soon as I hear anything. Thanks, Dr. Sawyer, for looking after that wee doll. I took quite a shine to her myself."

Troy put down the phone.

So, the police didn't know where they were. That wasn't the kind of news Troy had been hoping to hear.

He heard crying. He quickly headed for the living room.

Lucinda was wrapped tightly in the wool blanket. She must have rolled around in her crying. She was heading for the floor when he reached down to save her from the fall.

"I am here, Lucinda. You are okay." Troy was freeing her legs from the blanket. "Mama will be home soon." That was a lie. But he had to say something to stop her crying. Her sleepy whimper had progressed to heartbreaking sobs again.

"Do you want something to eat?" Troy headed for the kitchen with Lucinda. When he noticed the wet of Lucinda's bottom, he hadn't changed her since he picked her up from Audrey. He veered upstairs to change her instead. He washed her and changed her clothes.

Chapter Nineteen

Lionel was careening around another corner when he noticed a police car ahead. He slowed down so as not to overtake it. Diana was slumped down in the seat because Lionel had bashed her to stop screaming at the last red light. She had started screaming intensely in front of the people waiting for a bus. Several people had looked at the van questioningly, but he hoped that he had quietened her before they became overly curious.

Now, he was keeping an eye on the cop car ahead.

Lionel's mind detoured. Where was he going? Another town? He didn't have much money with him, stopping for gas will use that up. He looked around for a bank. There were only industrial buildings. Lionel noticed that the cop car had peeled off with its sirens going. He breathed a sigh of relief. Clearly, they weren't looking for him.

He saw a mall up ahead. Hopefully, there will be a bank. He spotted a self-serve gas station and stopped to get gas. Against his better judgment, he left Diana alone in the car. Her slumped body appeared unconscious. He locked the car so that she couldn't escape. After pumping the gas, he had glanced in at her. Not being able to see through the tinted glass, he unlocked the door. She still appeared unconscious. Then he softly closed the door, locking it. He went inside to pay for the gas.

Diana ended playing possum to peer out, no Lionel. She slipped into the driver's seat. No keys, oh no, he had taken the keys. She pressed the door lock release, grabbing the handle, she lifted it. The door opened, but Lionel's arm was there, thrusting her back inside. She had waited too long before acting on her escape. Diana screamed and Lionel hit her.

"Stop, you stupid bitch," pushing her away from behind the wheel. Diana pushed the horn. Lionel twisted her arm. "I don't know why I want you. You are not worth it. You have changed. Either you behave, or I will get rid of you over the next bridge or down some steep incline."

Diana rubbed her arm where he had twisted it. "Lionel, you can't keep me against my will. I will get away sometime when you are sleeping. You have to sleep sometime. I am hungry, aren't you going to feed me?" changing direction.

"I am hungry too, but I can't trust you to behave."

"I promise, Lionel. I need something in my stomach. I feel lightheaded."

"That is too bad. If you had come willingly, things would be different. But you had to fight me, didn't you?"

"Lionel, you left our baby stranded in a park. She is too young to fend for herself. How could you be so uncaring?"

He was so mad at her. He hit the side of her face leaving another welt from his ring.

"That child is not mine. I would never produce an imperfect child. How many times do I have to tell you that?"

"Lionel, you can deny her all you want, but she is your child. A helpless child that we left crying in the mud. How can you ever think I would live with you ever again when you treat my child like that?" She was wiping her face with the tips of her fingers, trying to ease the pain. They came away with blood on them.

"Lionel, please give up. The police will find you. They will hunt you down no matter where you go. It is a crime to abandon a child. Besides, now that I have started the divorce proceedings, I am officially not your wife, so this is no longer a domestic altercation. According to the police, I am not your wife. You have kidnapped me." Her voice was firm and full of bitterness.

"Diana, if I can't have you as my wife, I might as well end it right now." Lionel's voice was fierce.

"What do you mean, Lionel?" Fear eating at her. Did he mean he would do something to her or himself or both? She waited for his answer in dread. But he never answered her.

Her baby was out there somewhere. Had someone found her? Was she still alone? Hopefully not, and if the person who found Lucinda, would they let the police know? They wouldn't know who she was.

Then she calmed down. Audrey and Betty were there. She remembered seeing them look at Lionel's van, relief set in, but then dread hit her again. Her friends had turned away from the park after seeing the vehicle. Why had they done that? Did they go back to find Lucinda? If they did, would they phone the police? She was sure Audrey and Betty would share the care of Lucinda if they found her. She was getting desperate. *Please, God, save my baby.*

Diana's mind was so busy. She hadn't noticed that Lionel had pulled into a shopping mall until he pulled to a stop. They were near a bank. Good, he would have to leave her this time. Maybe she could get away or scream for help. Then the van started again. Lionel had spotted a drive-thru ATM machine.

Diana's hopes dropped into her boots. Why did there have to be a drive-thru? Would fate never be on her side today?

Lionel made three transactions from the machine, amounting to a fair bit of money. How much was enough? The more he was able to extract, the longer he could run. Lionel had been stuffing the bills into an inside pocket in his jacket. Then he zoomed away from the bank. There was a Wendy's down the line of stores at the end.

Diana knew that they had a drive-thru that required an attendant to deal with the cash. Maybe she could call out to them for help. When they pulled up to the message board, the voice asked for their order, and Diana yelled, "help me."

Lionel quickly laughed. "Cut out the clowning, Eve. This person doesn't have time for your silly antics." He gave the order. The voice said, "your order came to $16.20, so pull up at the next window."

He moved the van to the window indicated. Before the young girl could ask for the money, Lionel shoved a $20 bill out the crack of the window and told her to keep the change. "Put the order on the roof of the van. My wife has a contagious viral infection." Then Lionel whipped the window closed. He had done it so fast that Diana didn't have time to yell or scream.

She felt sure that they wouldn't believe her anyway after what he had said back at the order voice box.

When the food appeared and was placed on the roof, Lionel eased the van forward slowly until he cleared the window, then he quickly stepped out, grabbed the bags and tray of drinks, then dropped back into the vehicle. Diana managed to yell out, "help me." In a loving, laughing voice, Lionel said, "Eve, you are such a card, do you know that?" Slamming the door closed behind him as he shifted behind the wheel, thrusting the bags and drink tray at her. Diana grabbed the drink tray so the pop and juice would not tumble into her lap.

Lionel threw the van into gear and pulled out of the parking lot, squealing his tires. People looked at them in disgust. Probably, thinking that they were a bunch of punks doing wheelies.

"Lionel, I have to go to the washroom. Please stop. I need to go badly." She hated to plead with him, but she had no choice. She knew he wouldn't let her go off on her own.

He was racking his brain. How was he to handle this latest request for him to stop?

Then the answer came to him as he spotted a drive-in theater. Of course, he would take Diana to the drive-in. They had washrooms which you entered from outside. People would be busy watching the movie, or else they would be at the refreshment stand. They wouldn't even notice them. Pulling in quickly, Lionel paid for the tickets. Then the car slowly crept inside. He drew as close as he could to the washrooms without drawing attention to themselves.

Lionel observed that the picture was a mystery. No doubt, everyone was entranced with the plot. So, there wasn't anyone wandering around. That was unexpected luck.

Easing her out of the van, Lionel pushed her into the lady's washroom. He entered behind her and locked the door. There were two stalls. He waited until she went inside to relieve herself. Then he slipped into the other one. He would kill two birds with one stone. As soon as he heard her flush the toilet, he zipped his pants and headed out before her. Diana went to wash her hands while she looked at her face. It was showing colorful bruises already. There was swelling in places with blood trickling down where the ring had cut into her skin. She took a paper towel wetting it. She ran it gently over her face trying to remove the blood.

"Enough, Diana, come, we have to leave." He grasped her arm in a hammerlock, so she had to move with him. He unlocked the door and stuck out his head to check the area. Then pulled her out with him. He glanced at the screen.

The picture depicted a shadowy figure walking through the fog following the heroine, a frail blond girl encased in fear, her eyes dilated. People probably wondering how soon the shadow would catch her?

Thankfully, no one was wandering around.

Lionel opened the van to shove her inside. Her hope was gone as no one would save her if she screamed. No doubt they would think it was a part of the movie. He started the car, backing out of the spot where he had parked, and headed for the exit. Gone was her golden opportunity.

"Give me a hamburger. You better eat yours. Everything will be cold now because of you. I'll have a pop, so put a straw in one of the cups," he ordered.

They both ate from hunger because the food was indeed cold but tasty. Diana drank the apple juice.

"Lionel, we can't keep driving around. We will soon need sleep. Why don't you let me go? I won't talk to the police, I promise. I can never be your wife, ever again. Please, Lionel, let me go?"

"Diana, you are my wife until death do us part. Remember our wedding vows? Do not plead with me again. You are making me angry. Diana, obey your vows. That is all I ask of you. I will never let you divorce me. I know you are very friendly with Dr. Sawyer. Is he the reason you want a divorce?"

Diana looked at him in horror.

"Of course not. Dr. Sawyer is only a friend because I lived with his sister. I am still living in his sister's house. Why would you think such a thing? I'm getting a divorce because the police said they couldn't protect me from you unless we're officially separated or divorced. So, I took legal action against you as soon as I could afford it after you harassed me that night at the Inn."

"That is good that you are not involved with Dr. Sawyer. I would hate to think you would take your wedding vows so lightly as to commit adultery."

"Lionel, you broke your wedding vows when you denied your daughter, in my opinion. Our marriage was over as soon as you told your parents the baby died at birth. So, don't rant about me not living up to my wedding vows. How many times do I have to keep repeating myself before it sinks in?"

"Don't you ever talk to me like that again? Don't talk to me about that child either. I told you it isn't mine." This time he struck her so hard with his fist that she slumped over unconscious.

His anger was so intense when he observed her slumped body it didn't even bother him. At least now, she couldn't distract him with her mouthing off.

He glanced in the review mirror only to see a cop car on his tail. He wondered if the cop had recognized his van from a radio description.

The cruiser followed two cars back, never passing, never speeding up, just going with traffic flow. Were the cops tailing him, or was the cruiser on a regular patrol?

The only way to find out was to turn off at the first opportunity. He would turn off at the next light if that was possible. He kept driving, concentrating on traffic, awaiting the chance he needed.

Two blocks further on, he could see a traffic light. There were four cars in front of him. He needed the vehicles to get through the stoplight, but red for him. Could that scenario possibly happen? He doubted it.

The light was upon them. One car went through, then the second car delayed and went through with three, but the auto directly in front of him stopped as the stoplight changed to orange. Frequently, the driver ran the yellow light. It was just his bad luck, a cautious driver. Was there enough room between him and the curb to slip by the car? It would be close, but he had to try.

The van's wheels scraped the curb as he eased past the stopped car. He was going to make it around the corner. He hoped it was a long red light so that the patrol car was hemmed in for a while. Lionel speeded up a little as traffic on the street was light. He pulled away from the traffic light intersection with the gap widening.

But the answer came all too soon. The cop car had turned onto the street behind them. Lionel waited for the red and blue lights to start flashing and to hear the siren. But the cruiser never increased speed. Lionel lowered his speed to normal.

Lionel relaxed, thinking that this must be just a coincidence. He concentrated so much on the rearview mirror that he didn't watch the traffic ahead, not seeing that there were two police cruisers behind a truck in the oncoming traffic.

He was watching the mirror when a flash of a car invaded his peripheral vision. A patrol car had pulled over sideways in front of him. Lionel slammed on the brakes, wrenching the wheel away from it. In his panic, he stomped on the gas. The van shot over the curb. The car sailed through a plate glass window into a car dealership's showroom.

In its uncontrolled speed, the van caromed into the front of a brand-new Cadillac in shiny white and chrome exterior that noisily crunched as the van continued in an upward motion atop the Cadillac as the two vehicles met in a dance of death. The car salesmen's faces were shocked at the sight of metal meeting metal. The black monster had attacked and consumed the white Cadillac. Evil against good and evil won as the black van caromed to a stop atop the now twisted body of the once shiny new white Cadillac.

However, the bodies inside the van had not fared as well. Both Lionel and Diana were unconscious. The airbags had exploded, pinning them both in their place.

The police came rushing in. The salesmen were still frozen in place, staring at the damage to their beautiful showroom and that special car that was no more.

One of the officers climbed up on the passenger side. Fortunately, the Cadillac was wider than the van. The doors were locked with the engine still running. "Damned tinted glass. I can't see a thing," he yelled.

Another officer got up on the driver's side. This time the door opened but only partway as the framework was bent in the extensive collision caused by the black warrior of destruction. It was open enough that he managed to reach past the partially deflating airbag with his long slim arm and turn off the key to silence the beast.

The officer took out a knife to carve into the airbag, watching it shrivel as the air swished out, spreading a powdery substance. He reached for the release lock in the door for the passenger side.

The officer on the passenger side heard the lock release. He reached for the door, not expecting it to open because of the impact damage, but luckily it did.

The night air filled with sirens and the voices of the notable growing crowd of nosy gawkers that always gathered with the noise of chaos and destruction of twisted steel. A usually deserted neighborhood became a mass of gaping bodies wanting to see the gory carnage. Two officers were trying to contain them.

"C'mon, stay back. This vehicle may explode. We don't know about the gas tank. It may be leaking."

The throng moved back two feet.

"More, we need to get the emergency crew inside to deal with this. Come on, folks, back up. You can't see anything more unless we can get the teams of emergency personnel inside. The crowd moved back two more feet.

A burly fireman pushed his body through the thick mass of onlookers, making way for his comrades to gain entrance to the door of the once shiny bright, inviting showroom. The paramedics were trailing the firefighters with their emergency bags of medical equipment.

The officer had deflated the collapsing airbag on the passenger side, seeing an unconscious woman against the seat. The officer tried to assess her injuries when he realized the paramedics had reached the devastation and were behind him. He jumped down.

One paramedic immediately leaped into action, leaping onto the hood of the Cadillac. At the same time, the firefighters assessed their need to use the jaws of life to remove the driver. A young firefighter headed back to the fire truck with purpose written all over his face. The crowd parted to ease his path.

The paramedic took Diana's vital signs. Two firefighters were pouring foam under the van around the gas tank, just to be safe.

"John, I think this lady isn't too badly off. God must've protected her this night, or maybe she had already passed out before the carnage finished. Let's get her out of here and see."

Ralph released the belt and pushed the deflated airbag under the dashboard as best he could. He took the lady's shoulders and eased them forward to get his arm around her. Then slipped his other arm under her body. He was standing on the crushed roof of the Cadillac. He didn't have enough room to extract her.

"John, I can't do it. We will have to drag her out, which I didn't want to do until I was sure of her injuries. There isn't enough room to maneuver up here."

"Ralph, can you ease her shoulders out at least, so her body's upright?"

One of the salesmen standing nearby earlier had assessed the situation and now appeared with a wooden platform he carried along with another young man from the repair department, putting it in place. It was a decent width, so John quickly mounted the three steps to the platform and was able to grasp the victim's shoulders that were halfway out of the van.

"John, I can't maneuver around with my precarious footing. So, you will have to take her weight as you lift, and I'll try to ease her out. She is still unconscious, which makes her dead weight."

"Okay, Ralph, I have her." She slid down into his muscled arms. "Can you free her legs now? Okay, I've got her. Can you guide my steps as I turn? I don't want to fall off the steps, as I can't see my feet."

Ralph started to give directions when a burly firefighter appeared on the step, one step off the floor with extended arms. Diana slid into his arms. He stepped down and turned to carry her to a vacant place on the marble floor. The two paramedics jumped down the last couple of steps. They were with her instantly, feeling her body for injuries. Again, they could find none that were apparent other than facial wounds. It looked like the man had abused her from the dried blood. Then John noticed her nose. It appeared twisted, a broken nose probably from the airbag. It was miraculous that she had gotten off so easy.

"Ralph, I believe she must have been unconscious at impact. She came out unscathed except for her nose. The facial damage looks like he had been hitting her. The rat," he ended fervently.

John retook her vital signs. Ralph and a firefighter waded through the crowd to get to the stretcher. It was easier this time because the police had moved most of the mob away from the door. The gawkers wanted to see the twisted metal more than the victims. The officers had guided the group towards the space back from the broken window.

Another fire truck appeared with its lights flashing and sirens wailing. Firefighters were leaping down before it came to a complete stop. They could see their comrades working inside the showroom through the wide-open space where the window had been. The glass fragments were now covering the floor and the vehicles. They could see that the van door was almost off.

The captain quickly assessed the situation. He got two of his men with large heavy-duty brooms to clear the glass and two others to remove the shards of lethal pointed glass still adhered to the window frame before anyone got hurt. The crowd was again trying to push closer. The rest of the firefighters physically overpowered the group with the bulk of their heavy boots, bulky coats, and hard helmets, easing the crowd back out of harm's way. They were brooking no resistance.

Diana was lifted gently by four men onto the stretcher that had arrived. She was still unconscious. The paramedics strapped her in. Then one headed out to the ambulance with the help of a firefighter. He was going to sit with Diana while the paramedic went back to help the male victim. The paramedics had not wanted to leave Diana alone while still unconscious and capable of choking or going into shock when she regained consciousness.

Standing on ladders, the firefighters had the van's door removed enough, but there wasn't room for the platform. So, they would have to ease him out flat on the seat and extract him from the passenger side. They hadn't been able to assess his injuries. One paramedic climbed in from the passenger side. The male victim groaned as the paramedic tried to move him, so he wasn't dead, only unconscious.

Ralph called out all of Lionel's injuries that he could see. "The right leg is at a funny angle, so it is evident the leg is broken, and his right arm too. His left leg has a prosthesis. There is a gash on the side of his neck. It appears the belt buckle gave way on impact, releasing the belt, and the buckle must have swung up to strike his neck. It is now resting on his shoulder. The only conclusion I can come to about the seatbelt is that the victim really must have been violently tossed about on impact. Perhaps his airbag was late in deploying, or he hadn't engaged the seatbelt properly for some reason. Regardless of how it happened, the guy is lucky he wasn't killed by it."

The paramedic decided the easiest way to remove him was head first, hoping that his legs would follow without jamming. They tried, but his legs were not cooperating.

The only blessing was the undercarriage had embedded itself into the twisted car below so that the van didn't move during all of these activities.

The firefighters who released the door had removed the ladders and equipment back to the truck, knowing they were removing the injured victim from the passenger side.

When Ralph was having trouble extracting Lionel because his legs were so injured, a firefighter offered to get a ladder for the driver's side.

John said, "Don't bother." He threw a rope to Ralph from the pile on the floor. A firefighter managed to climb up the rope that Ralph had hooked onto the passenger side's door, then slung over the roof to hang down. He stepped onto the top of the lower car.

The firefighter was to aid the victim's legs in exiting the van. He took care to remove the limbs slowly.

The victim was clear of the wreck, leaving the firefighter suspended on the rope. He went to shimmy down the rope when there was a grinding noise. The moving weight on the line pulled the van sideways with a grinding squeal with the separation of the two vehicles. The man fell to the floor, but not before the door, mostly pried off, separated on impact with the wall, and hit his helmet. Then bounced off, hitting his shoulder, breaking the bone with its sharp edge, leaving the van precariously wedged against the wall.

The other two firefighters managed to duck.

Everyone knew then that they should have secured the two vehicles with ropes, but the cars had seemed firmly embedded together.

All had given their first concern to the victims. It would appear that the weight of the firefighter on the rope managed to unbalance the van and tear the twisted metal clear after the weight of Lionel's body was removed.

The captain quickly radioed for another ambulance and tow trucks to remove the two vehicles from their precarious positions. The two firefighters, having ducked, crawled out with the injured man from under the van wedged against the wall, stopping all three men from being killed or crushed.

After stabilizing Lionel, by immobilizing his leg and his arm, they lifted him onto the stretcher that had arrived. The paramedics were looking at the injured firefighter to see if they could do anything for him. They heard the fast-approaching sirens of the other ambulance's arrival. So, the two paramedics left the firefighter's side to load Lionel's stretcher and head for the hospital.

When they got to the ambulance, the firefighter jumped down. He said, "she isn't fully conscious, but she moaned a couple of times."

"We had better get going to the hospital." Lionel's stretcher was squeezed in place, barely room for the attendant. John hopped out to get the ambulance moving. He transmitted that their ETA would be ten minutes upon noting that traffic was reasonably light. They arrived in record time. The two stretchers were quickly transferred into the Emergency.

Chapter Twenty

The phone rang. Lucinda had been sleeping more deeply but awoke with the sound of the ringing. When Troy whipped her up in his arms, Lucinda grabbed hold of his neck tightly. Troy headed to the phone with a hopeful heart.

"Hello."

"Dr. Sawyer, this is Officer Jackson. Word has just come in. Mrs. Cardwell and her husband or her ex, I guess, have arrived at West Minister Hospital after a car crash. They went off the road into a showroom of a car dealership. There is no word of their injuries as of yet. I thought you would like to know. All I know is that her injuries are not life threatening."

"Thank you. We will get over there immediately. Thank you, I appreciate your calling me."

"You're welcome, Dr. Sawyer. I took an interest in this case after the situation at the hospital when the baby was born. I would like there be a happy ending for the mother and baby, this time."

"Me too. I will go there now." Troy hung up the phone. He headed upstairs to change Lucinda. She was lying placidly against his body, her head resting on his shoulder. Her thumb was firmly installed in her mouth. This new habit was part of her now.

The trip to the hospital was as speedy as traffic allowed. Lucinda was strapped in beside him inside a big blanket because he had no baby car seat for her. A few months ago, he had removed it when he was transporting a few of his colleagues to a conference. He had not needed to reinstall it in the back seat. He worried for her safety, hoping that being bundled up in a blanket would protect her.

Troy talked incessantly to her about her mommy, mentioning that they were heading to the hospital to find her. Troy was comforting Lucinda, and hoping he could reassure himself in the process. He had no idea what he would find when he got there. Troy just knew that he loved Diana. He intended to declare his love for her at the first possible moment. Diana has been in two car accidents, and surviving was not anything but a miracle. He needed to tell her that he loved her for his sake as much as hers. Could or would she share his feelings? He had no idea, even though he knew her marriage was not something she wanted anymore. Regardless, he still intended to regale her with his love. He hoped she was ready to accept him this time.

Lucinda was repeating, "Mama, Mama," in a teary voice. No child should be separated from their mother, the way Lionel had done. Troy was glad that he had been the prominent male figure in Lucinda's life. She was comfortable with him. He liked the fact that she had called him 'Dada' as soon as she could talk. Troy really did want to be her daddy. He wanted and intended to adopt her. Hopefully, he could convince Diana to become his wife after the divorce was final. Troy certainly wished that he could speed up that process.

He wondered what stage their relationship would be in if Diana had agreed to come to his place? What if Lucy sold the house? Be realistic, Troy. Diana wouldn't have moved in with you in the first place. Oh well, wishful thinking helps me keep going.

The trip to the hospital was over. There it was on the next corner. What would he find? How badly would she be injured? Would she be willing to share his love? He had never wished for anything so much.

Troy would like to string Lionel up for the pain he has inflicted on his wife and child. Surely the police could do something more to protect her this time? They couldn't keep ignoring the situation.

Diana needs protection against a man who is no longer her husband but in name only. How often could she keep being in accidents and survive? Each time he has kidnapped her, it has ended in an accident. He was dreading what he would find when he got inside. How badly was Diana injured? Had Lionel died this time?

He parked the car. Troy gathered Lucinda up into his arms, removing her from the protective blanket. Lucinda instantly clung to him.

"We are going to find mommy. She is inside this building." His feet carried him through the automatic doors to the desk.

"Can I help you?"

"Yes, I am Dr. Sawyer. I am looking for Diana Cardwell. She came in from a vehicle accident. A van went through a plate-glass window into a car dealership's showroom."

"Yes, Dr. Sawyer. There were two victims. One is in surgery and the other is in cubicle seven. That patient is on their way to OR and maybe has already gone. You can ask at the nurse's station down that corridor over there." Pointing in the general direction to the other side of the Emergency. "They will have more up-to-date information."

Troy knew the fact that he was a doctor was getting him through some of the red tape. He needed that right now and walked over to the other side of Emergency.

"Can you tell me the condition of Diana Cardwell? I am Dr. Sawyer, a family friend. This is her baby." The nurse at the desk looked at them with interest. They usually only gave information to the immediate family at this point.

Troy gave her an intent look. Lucinda started to whimper like she didn't want to be here amongst this hustle and bustle of wheelchairs, stretchers, people with blood on them, and others with bandages.

"Dr. Sawyer, I don't have any details of her injuries. I just know that she is waiting outside the OR for an operating room to take care of her injuries. She is down this corridor in the holding area. We don't let anyone down there except emergency personnel. If you want more information, speak to the nurse that worked with the doctor that examined her. She would know more."

Troy turned away with a thank you. He whipped back towards Emergency. He had to find out what was going on. He had to.

"Mommy's here. baby, and we will find her." He tightened his arms around Lucinda. As if to shield her from the surroundings and to comfort her. His pace quickened in his desperate need for more information as to the extent of Diana's injuries.

She must not be too bad, or she would have been rushed in immediately. So, it must be Lionel in OR. Would they save him? What was the extent of his injuries? Troy wanted the man contained and away from Diana, but he certainly didn't want his death. Troy was a doctor who saved lives, not desiring them destroyed.

If Troy hadn't had Lucinda, he knew that he would have blended in using his status as a doctor to get into places. But Lucinda made it evident that he wasn't here on duty, but only as a visitor awaiting details of a loved one.

His search was finally successful after asking many nurses. He found the right one.

"Can you tell me anything about Mrs. Cardwell? What are her injuries? I am Dr. Sawyer, and this is her baby." Using the last two comments in the hopes that she would be more forthcoming with information.

"Doctor, Mrs. Cardwell, has gone to OR. She needs bones set in her left wrist, and her nose needs attention. The wrist is definitely broken. Deployment of the airbags does that sometimes. They save the patient's life, but their sudden forceful explosion does break bones. We have found that. At least, I am assuming that was what broke her wrist. We have seen this happen fairly frequently. Better a broken bone than death through the windshield." She paused before she gave him a second message about the patient.

"The doctor felt that Mrs. Cardwell was unconscious when the accident happened. It was evident that her bloody facial abrasions were caused by a sharp-edged ring on someone's fist. He also said that he felt that being unconscious probably saved her from further serious injuries."

Troy was relieved that her bones would heal, and there were no life-threatening injuries, thankfully. He would just have to be patient. He wasn't happy to hear about the abrasions.

"Do you know what her ex-husband's condition is?"

"Sorry, Dr. Sawyer. I didn't deal with him. I only know that he went directly into the OR ahead of Mrs. Cardwell." She quickly walked away. She was too busy to linger any longer.

Troy went back to the waiting room. He had to find Lucinda something to drink. He had grabbed a bottle out of the cupboard in case he needed it.

Then he changed his mind. He needed to locate the cafeteria to get some milk because emergency waiting areas only had coffee and pop machines.

The cafeteria would take up some time while Diana was in the OR. Lucinda was back to sucking her thumb. Troy hadn't fed her for a while, and milk would sustain her until he got her home.

It was late and past the dinner hour, so the cafeteria wasn't too busy. Troy went over to the counter. A pleasant woman behind the counter display of fruits and desserts asked if she could help him.

"I wonder if you could fill this bottle with warm milk? It would be better for her than cold milk. Do you mind?"

"No, we aren't too busy. It won't be a problem."

She looked at him with interest, an attractive man and a cute baby. All the nice ones were married. She reasoned as she went through the process of filling the bottle from a carton of milk. She placed the bottle in the microwave for a few seconds. Then shook it so the milk was evenly heated. From experience, she knew that the microwave sometimes made areas in the liquid too high a temperature, which can cause anyone trying to consume it to burn their mouth. She automatically tested it on her wrist, having had three children of her own.

It felt warm but not hot. Again, the woman liked the look of this man as she walked towards him. His winning smile was contagious. Andrea usually didn't notice men. But for some reason, this man drew her attention. It was odd because she hadn't thought about men and relationships since Greg had died. Maybe her period of mourning was finally over. It had been three years since Greg's death. She was thankful now that she had noticed him in this way.

Andrea held out the heated milk. Lucinda immediately reached for the bottle, which Troy now retained in his grip for safety's sake? One thing about getting it filled here was that the staff wore plastic gloves for health reasons. He felt confident giving Lucinda a bottle that would still be sterile.

Troy paid the cashier for the milk while he balanced Lucinda. She was sucking noisily on the bottle in her haste to fill her empty stomach.

He walked to an empty table to sit with comfort while Lucinda drained the bottle. Troy looked down at her. His heart expanded with pleasure having her in his arms.

But then his thoughts went quickly to Diana. She would need help now that she would be in a cast again.

Perhaps, he should move into Lucy's old bedroom. Diana had never moved into the master bedroom, even after Lucy got married and moved. Diana always thought of that as Lucy's room.

Troy knew Diana would fight his moving in for convention's sake. But he intended to be adamant and disarm her resistance for her benefit.

Lucinda had finished her bottle. He recapped the empty bottle and returned it to the diaper bag. Troy looked like an actual father as he handled Lucinda. Several women glanced in his direction with interest, a male mother. Was his wife having another baby? Was that why these two were here? Some looked at him with sensual desire. Troy's only interest was Lucinda and her mother being oblivious to the others around him.

He hoped that Diana would be released to go home by the time he got back to Emergency. He had called Lucy to fill her in. She offered to come back and help with Diana and Lucinda's care. Troy dodged answering Lucy because he wanted to play that vital role in Diana's recovery. He had run out of patience with his brotherly role. Troy wanted to announce to the world that he loved Diana but instead was willing to play the role of a brother still to be in on Diana's recovery.

These thoughts paraded through his mind as he walked back to Emergency. Lucinda was resting on his broad comfortable shoulder.

Troy tried again by going to the nurse's station in the OR corridor.

"Is Mrs. Cardwell out of OR?"

"Yes, she is in room 325 on the third floor."

"Why?" he hadn't expected that. Diana's injuries had sounded minor.

"Her injuries must have indicated that she needed to stay at least overnight. The nurse on the third floor will be able to give you more details." She smiled reassuringly at him. Now, Troy saw life from a different angle from a doctor. Information took patience and worry for a loved one. It was shaping his viewpoint of hospital life in another direction.

Troy went to find the elevator. He was glad Lucinda had gone to sleep after her bottle. He felt sad for a woman carrying a squalling baby as she passed.

Then his mind swung to Diana. Why were they keeping her overnight? Was she worse than first reported to him?

The snail's pace elevator finally opened on the third floor. The doors trudged back reluctantly, it seemed. Troy wasn't patient. He hit the floor at a fast pace. The words were spilling out as he cornered a nurse.

"What is Mrs. Cardwell's condition? She came up from OR." Smiling was difficult when he was impatient for an answer.

"She is in room 325. She is here for observation only. She has a cast on her broken wrist. From the chart, I think the observation period is because of the trauma she has been through. You can go in to see her. Your wife is sedated. So, she might be asleep." She smiled encouragingly at him. Troy showed his relief that Diana's injuries were no worse than were first indicated to him.

Troy quickened his steps in anticipation of finally being able to see Diana for himself. The sound of the bell as he walked through the door indicated visiting hours were over. The room contained two beds. A man was rising to kiss his wife, and Troy presumed she had an injured leg under a blanket tent. So, Troy swung his eyes to the other bed. There was Diana. Her face showed evidence of bruising and cuts.

The fresh abrasions were the same type caused by Lionel's ring at the last kidnapping. Troy's chest almost caved in with pain. He had witnessed Lionel's marks before, which seemed to be his trademark. Was Diana's uncooperative behavior the reason? He wanted to go over to kiss each abrasion better.

Diana's closed eyes under the sedative she had received was evident in her deep sleep. He stood there, drinking in her beauty. However, she wasn't truly beautiful with the marred face at the moment. He wanted to kiss her. But he didn't think he should take that liberty while she was unaware. Lucinda was not going to wait. She wanted her mother, who had abandoned her at the playground.

Chapter Twenty-One

"Mama," cried Lucinda loudly as she wiggled anxiously to get to her mother. "Mama." Tears were forming from Troy's restrain and from her need for her mother.

Diane's eyes fluttered open, then closed. Her mind was trying to fight off the blackness. *Lucinda, my baby. You're here.* Her eyes fluttered open for a few seconds, then closed. *I want to see my baby. Please let me wake up.*

Lucinda was crying in earnest. Her Mommy wasn't responding to her the way she wanted. Troy was trying to soothe Lucinda, but she was solely rivetted on her mother, and nothing could deter her. She was fighting his embrace, bringing her knees up and pushing away with her knees, and her arms were thrown backward and pivoting.

Troy concentrated on controlling Lucinda's body before she fell. He tried to soothe her with promises that Mommy would wake up that her Mama wanted to be there for her.

Diana could hear Troy's voice. She could hear Lucinda's cries of "Mama, Mama." Her mind was becoming clearer. She fought hard for both their sakes. Her eyes popped open. She held out one arm because her other one was still aching. As Troy bent over, she touched her baby's hand that waved towards her, wanting closer.

"Diana, how are you? Lucinda has been hard to restrain since she saw you." Troy bent closer, so Diana could reach her daughter's face to trace its sweetness. The daughter she had thought she had lost forever. Remembering her baby crying inconsolably as Lionel dragged her away. The memory would be with her for a long time to come.

Diana's teary voice said, "Lucinda, Mama's here. Mama loves you. Can I have her, Troy?"

"Are you alright?" his voice held apprehension.

"Yes, please, Troy, I need her in my arms." Troy placed the squiggling baby, anxious to be held by her mother, in Diana's right arm. Lucinda cuddled into her sobbing, hitting at her mother's face in agitation.

Troy grabbed her hands and placed them both against Diana's cheek. Troy needed the contact as much as Lucinda. Diana felt the hands against her cheek, feeling the little hands embraced in Troy's larger hands, cupping her cheek lovingly.

Lucinda's hands withdrew, lying comfortably in her mother's arm at last. Troy and Diana's eyes met, showing their need. The motion of her cheek against his caressing hand spoke of the love they had for each other. Each thankful that they were together safely.

The moment called for a declaration as their eyes focused on each other. Their yearnings were no longer hidden.

"Diana, I love you," his voice husky at her reaction to him.

"Troy!" Diana exclaimed.

Lucinda had fallen asleep. She was safe in the arms of her loving Mama.

Diana and Troy wanted to express their need for each other.

Troy broke the contact of their eyes as his eyes fell to his hand against Diana's cheek. Her cheek caressed him in return. He leaned down, kissing her lips. The kiss was declaring their feelings for each other. Something neither could hide ever again.

The fear they had experienced from being apart during the past few hours and the possibility of losing each other stripped their reluctance. Their lips were melding together in love, not able to deny their passion any longer. They wished to embrace each other, knowing it was out of the question with a sleeping child in one arm and the cast on her broken wrist.

Troy slid his lips over to the sleeping child with abundant love for the child and Diana. Could these two ever be his? He wanted them in his life, in his home, in his arms forever.

He released his hand from her cheek with a caress, reaching for the button to raise the bed. Then he sat beside them and leaned over to put his hands on her face drawing her towards him for another kiss. The moan was hardly heard as their lips fused in an ever-deepening kiss. Their love exposed to each other at last.

A slight cough drew them apart unwillingly. The couple's yearning eyes were still clinging, although they moved apart reluctantly.

"My patient is supposed to be sleeping. But I think your therapy is the kind that I would prefer too." The nurse said with a little chuckle.

Diana blushed. But Troy didn't break the contact of their eyes as he said, "can't you leave and come back later?"

Again, the nurse chuckled. "Ten minutes, then you and the baby are gone. She is here for sedation, not seduction." This time the chuckle was a definite laugh with a bit of envy showing in her voice. Her rubber-sounding steps exited the room.

Barely above a whisper, Troy said, "I love you, Diana. I love you both very much." He patted Lucinda's hair trailing his fingers down her tear-stained face. Then he raised his hands to cup Diana's face, bonding their lips in love.

When they finally broke the fusion of their lips, Diana whispered, "I love you too, Troy. But I am still not free."

Then the thought hit her. "How is Lionel?"

"Why do you care?" Troy inquired bitterly.

"Because he is a human being. Despite my dislike of him now. I need to know about his condition."

"Diana, I understand that your gentle nature requires you to know. Perhaps the nurse could find out for you. Now I want to kiss you once more, as we have to leave for tonight. We will be back early tomorrow. I will stay at your place while you're here, for Lucinda's sake. I still have the key Lucy gave me long ago," he said in explanation.

"I don't want to let her go. Troy, it was terrible seeing her crawling on the ground sobbing as Lionel half carried, half dragged me away. I will never forgive him for that. It tore my heart out." The tears slid down her cheeks. Troy kissed them away.

"How did you find Lucinda?"

"Betty called me. She and Audrey found her and called the police."

"I saw them turn away from the park and dreaded that they wouldn't find Lucinda." The hurt in her voice was quite prevalent. "I thought she was gone forever."

"I will make it up to you. I will keep you two together forever if you let me."

"I know, but I am not free. Please ask me again if I ever get free. I love you, Troy, with all my heart," said Diana plaintively.

He wanted to say that it didn't matter that she wasn't free. At least not to him, but he knew how this gentle lady felt about life, and it did matter to her. He gave her a parting light kiss, after which he reached for the sleeping Lucinda, whom Diana reluctantly released.

Diana watched as Troy cuddled her sleeping child protectively into his shoulder. Lucinda's thumb entered her mouth, making a sucking sound as she settled against him.

"She is sucking her thumb," said Diana astonished.

"Yes, she started it after she left the park where she was left alone. I didn't have the heart to stop her. We had better go. Rest, my love, so that we can take you home tomorrow. Sweet dreams with my love surrounding you."

He turned away as the nurse appeared at the door. The nurse knew this woman's husband was in the accident. But she could also tell that these two were deeply in love. She wondered what their story was. Troy looked like the child's natural father. The way he was holding her against him and the mother looking after them both longingly.

Troy went to the Emergency desk. He asked the nurse on the OR hall how Lionel had fared, introducing himself as Dr. Sawyer.

She replied, "Mr. Cardwell is now in ICU. He has had a heart attack, leg injury, plus a broken arm.

Troy examined his feelings on this news. The heart attack was unexpected. That news was something he didn't feel would bode well for him.

Troy thanked the nurse. He left the hospital to take Lucinda home, his child, if only in his mind. He intended to adopt her as soon as possible so that Lucinda could have his name and love.

When Diana heard about Lionel being in ICU after a heart attack, Troy doubted that there would be any more declarations of love until she was free by divorce. The sadness of their fate set in. Their love would be put on hold.

But he still hoped someday Diana and Lucinda would be with him, surrounded by his caring and love.

**

Just as Troy suspected, Diana was quite distant the next day except with Lucinda. She asked him if he knew how she could get someone to stay with her for a while until her wrist started to heal. The writing was on the wall. She was putting distance between them once again without discussing Lionel. But he felt sure that she knew his condition because it hung there between them like a black cloud.

His own hopes were dashed. *Would Diana continue with the divorce now? Did Lionel having a heart attack change things? Would their feelings have to be put aside indefinitely?* Bleakness invaded his heart.

Troy made inquiries for a live-in companion as soon as they arrived at the house.

He knew that he at least had her for the day and night because Mrs. Owens couldn't come on such short notice, not until the next day.

Troy had moved his schedule around with the aid of his nursing assistant, so he was free today to help Diana with Lucinda. They could be a pretend family for one day.

Diana, who had gone through this once before, was adapting to her one-handed existence. She couldn't handle everything, so she was still dependent on Troy. Now that Lucinda had her Mama back, she wanted to be cuddled by Diana constantly.

Troy was close by to be helpful if needed. He made their meals and prepared Lucinda for her nap after changing her. He also bathed and put Lucinda to bed for the night.

During the day, Lucinda had been calling him 'dada.' This bolstered Troy's heart, and Diana seemed to cringe each time she heard 'dada.' He didn't know if it was because she dreaded the future. Guilt maybe, as she knew it wasn't to be because of her principles about being free from Lionel.

After Lucinda was down for the night, Troy brought Diana a cup of tea. They relaxed in front of the TV. But neither concentrated on the game show that gave off squeals of delight each time the petite teenager gave the correct answer.

Troy was glancing mostly at Diana. He told himself that he was checking to see if her face was showing signs of pain. Troy knew that this was a fabrication. He just wanted to gaze at her with the hope that she would someday be his.

Diana was deep in thought also. *Lionel was worse off than ever now that he had a heart attack. Could she continue with the divorce now that Lionel was incapacitated?*

Diana's next words hit him below the belt. "Troy, I am going to tell my lawyer to stop the divorce. I can't divorce Lionel now that he has had a heart attack. Lionel was so upset with me. If I continue, it might finish him. I couldn't live with that on my conscience. What kind of life could I live knowing that I was partially responsible for his death?"

She paused, giving him a look of sadness. Then continued as if to herself. "No, I couldn't live in happiness after I did that."

Troy's fears were drawn into reality. It wasn't what he wanted to hear. He loved this woman all the more for her gentle convictions. Her refusal to let him have the family he dearly wanted left him anguished.

"Diana, I respect you too much to argue, but will you go back to Lionel after all that has happened?"

"No, but I can't add to Lionel's problems by divorcing him when he is so dead set against it. It could indeed cause his death if the divorce ever became final. His life without me is so dreadful, he says. That was why he captured me again."

She continued. "Troy, please understand I couldn't share your love the way you and I want if Lionel's death hung there between us."

"I know Diana, but I hope he recovers quickly. Then maybe we will have a chance. Please wait. Just tell your lawyer to put the divorce on hold until Lionel's recovery."

"I'll think about it."

Squeals from the TV drew their eyes. The loud lamenting, screeching blaring coming out from the TV, as the petite blond had won the top prize. Both of them seeing and hearing but without interest as the TV cut to a commercial.

Diana declared, "I think I will go to bed now. I don't feel like any more TV tonight."

Troy leaped up to help her. She gracefully accepted his help, knowing she would need his aid to retire as well. She sent him for pain pills as soon as they reached the bedroom. She undressed, but her progress was too cumbersome. She felt exposed when he returned.

Troy knew her predicament. He kept his eyes on her face, handing her the pills and water, watching her as the pills disappeared into her mouth like a dutiful patient.

"Diana, I am going to help you undress. I am a doctor. Could you think of me that way? Please, I want to help you. Your arm is hurting you too much to be harassing yourself unnecessarily with actions of undressing."

His hands were quite impersonal as he helped her while his heart pounded against his wishes, but he had to put his feelings aside until Diana was willing.

Diana's face was quite pink over his dressing her. She headed for the bedroom. Knowing she was embarrassed, he said, "Goodnight."

Troy knew she would prefer it that way.

The next day Mrs. Owens arrived. Troy whipped Diana into his arms to speed her descent on the stairs, knowing that she would prefer to greet Mrs. Owens. The way her body stiffened spoke volumes to him, confirming Diana's message from last night. Troy knew there was no point in his staying. Diana was still committed to Lionel legally.

They greeted Mrs. Owens. Troy grabbed the door handle.

"I had better be going. I have a busy day ahead of me. Goodbye, Diana." He leaned towards her to kiss her, but it landed on her cheek instead of meeting her lips. Diana's further message to him, no divorce, no love acknowledgment, his heart sunk, and so did hers.

Chapter Twenty-Two

Six Months Later

Diana was at the park with Audrey and Betty, along with their children. Audrey and Betty were trying to motivate her into continuing the divorce.

"What about Dr. Sawyer? Are you still seeing him?" Audrey queried, expecting a yes.

"I guess I burnt my bridges there. I informed Troy to quit calling after my decision not to divorce Lionel. I felt it was unfair to him to keep him coming around. It was hurting us both, being in a hopeless love situation. Lucinda misses him so much." Diana wanted to insert, *and so do I.*

Diana paused with regret that their love couldn't be. Then she went on.

"It wasn't fair to Dr. Sawyer to keep him in limbo. But it hurt my daughter a great deal when he finally stopped coming."

"Besides, I heard from Lucy. He is seeing someone else." Diana tried to keep the sadness at bay by smiling brightly. "I hope he has a good life. I also hope his new lady makes him happy."

"Yeah, right," said Audrey. "You should call him. You need to know if there is another lady in his life for sure. You owe that to yourself and Lucinda too. Encourage him to come and see Lucinda. He would come if only you summoned him."

"No, I can't." Diane picked up Lucinda and put her in the stroller. She had to get away from these two friends who were trying to raise her hopes, but she knew it was hopeless.

She had her job at the Castleton Inn. She had a roof over her head with a comfortable life once Troy stopped coming.

Lucinda was looking towards the road. Diana turned to see what she was looking at.

It was Lionel. He was there coming towards them. Diana's heart did a topsy turvy.

Lionel rolled into the park. A nurse pushed his wheelchair to where Diana and her two friends were standing.

At the sight of Lionel, everyone panicked. Betty regained her cool and turned away to call Troy. She whispered into the phone, "Lionel is here. Listen," she said, and Troy's body tightened as he stood listening.

Lionel was bold and brash as he directed his nurse to push him up to Diana. She quickly grabbed up Lucinda, clutching her tightly against her body.

The nurse stood behind the wheelchair with a smirk on her face and defiance in her stance.

"Diana," Lionel growled, "you have been a pathetic wife and a great disappointment to me. Your child is not acceptable to me, and I find no reason to allow you into my home ever again."

Diana looked at him blankly, then looked at her friends, who were also looking dumbly at Lionel.

"In case you haven't noticed, I have found a much more suitable person to be my wife." The three women looked around, searching. Then their eyes swung back to focus on the nurse behind Lionel.

"Yes," bragged Lionel, "this is Sheila. She is well educated and more than able to care for me in the way that I deserve. She is also much more attractive than you ever were."

His voice changed to a sneer, "You have always been too skinny and frail. You are a pathetic person. It upsets me to think I wasted my time and injured my body for the likes of you. Never again will I see you."

Sheila stood tall, a grin spread across her face with each sentence of verbal abuse, as she looked down at Diana.

"In any event," Lionel continued, "you are not good enough for me. I want a divorce, and I want it now."

Diana's eyes opened wide in amazement as her arms tightened around Lucinda. Quietly she murmured, "of course, Lionel, as usual, you are right. I need to let you go. I will do as you wish."

"Good," he said, "good." Lionel looked up at Sheila in triumph. Sheila was patting his shoulders possessively. Then she grabbed the handles of the wheelchair, and they rolled away together without a goodbye.

Diana stood quietly as Lionel and Sheila drove away. Then the air was shattered as they all shouted in joy. Diana was soon to be free of Lionel at last. Her face wreathed in smiles of happiness.

They were so excited about Diana's freedom that they had not noticed Troy's arrival.

"Dada." Lucinda's outstretched arms were pleading. Troy walked past everyone to Diana's side. He seized Lucinda into his arms. Lucinda gave him smacking kisses in delight at seeing him. She kept saying Dada between kisses.

Troy was laughing at her exuberance as he turned to Diana.

"Hello, Diana."

"Hello, Troy." She could hardly contain her excitement at seeing him. "What are you doing here?"

"I have come to collect my family. The family that can be mine at last."

"How did you know about the divorce?" Diana's eyes whizzed over toward Audrey and Betty.

Betty held up her cell phone and turned it off. "I guess he didn't wait to hear all that Lionel had to say."

"I admit I only heard part of Lionel's speech. Then I zoomed over here. Do you mind, Diana?" Troy waited with expectation. He was waiting for her to say no, or was it too late?

"No, I don't mind," Diana whispered breathlessly.

Troy closed the gap between them. He gathered Diana into his arms, kissing her lovingly. Lucinda gave each a smacking kiss on their cheeks as Diana and Troy kissed with all their craving released at last.

Audrey and Betty were watching with broad smiles. The sight of these three people bonding together as a complete loving family spoke to each of the ladies' romantic sides. They beamed at the loving couple and their baby, proud that they accomplished the reunion for Diana.

Diana had yearned for Troy for far too long, and now it was viable. Audrey gave Betty a thumbs up for her quick phone call to Troy on sighting Lionel.

Soon there would be a loving father for Lucinda and a loving husband for Diana. A wedding that Audrey and Betty would be proud to celebrate with them.

The couple broke from the kiss that confirmed their future. Troy and Diana's openly declared devotion sealed the path towards a momentous future. Each kissed Lucinda, their daughter, to validate their family commitment with love.

Thanks for reading *Down and Out Pray*.
You can find my other works on my website.
www.dorothycollins.ca

CPSIA information can be obtained
at www.ICGtesting.com
Printed in the USA
BVHW080953160122
625815BV00003B/15